TEAPOTS

HI HO HI HO

TEAPOTS

TINA M. CARTER

Eagle
Editions

A QUANTUM BOOK

Published by Eagle Editions Ltd
11 Heathfield
Royston
Hertfordshire SG8 5BW

This edition printed 2002

ISBN 1-86160-507-2

QUMTEP

This book is produced by
Quantum Publishing
6 Blundell Street
London N7 9BH

Printed in Singapore by
Star Standard Industries Pte Ltd

CONTENTS

INTRODUCTION

Whether you have one favourite teapot for brewing tea or a collection that continues to grow, you will find this book an informative guide for both the general and special interest collector.

While collecting is very subjective, collectors spending anywhere from a few pounds up to £1,000 fall into two groups: generalist or specialist.

After finding there is something about teapots they just cannot resist, many collectors decide upon a certain category that is personally appealing, and specialize in collecting only those within that range. It may be teapots of a certain manufacturer, shape, material, colour, size, or other particular type. For example, many collectors specialize in Hall China teapots, while others seek only children's or toy tea sets.

The majority of teapot collectors are generalists who collect more by visual appeal and price rather than by category. Their collections include a wide variety of teapots, and the individual pots have their own unique

ABOVE LEFT ***Cobalt blue net design teapot*** **was made in Russia and is marked in script red letters: "A L B". It was purchased from the Lomonosov Factory, near Leningrad, well known for its classic blue and white porcelain. Matching cups are available, all from Horchow.**

ABOVE ***Blue and white china*** **teapot with the handle over the top. This pot was bought in Battle in England – the place where the Battle of Hastings was fought in 1066.**

RIGHT ***Airflow shape*** **was first introduced in 1940, and has been made periodically since then in various colours and decorations. It was re-issued in 1985. A decorated version with autumn leaves is currently available from China Specialties.**

BELOW ***Peasant woman*** **pours tea from the jug she carries. She was made in the U.S. c.1940 by Redwing, and is glazed in a creamy yellow. She is 8½ in/21.6 cm high and 10 in/ 25.4 cm wide. Other figural teapots made by Redwing include a rooster and a pumpkin.**

ABOVE ***Mini-Cadogan*** **teapot has an opening on the bottom for filling, and once the liquid is poured in and the teapot stood upright, the liquid remains in the teapot's chambers. Various versions of this little pot have been made – this one has a mouse on top. It is stamped on the bottom "Made in China". It has been suggested that these pots were made to hold soy sauce at the table.**

attraction or value. Often generalists have "collections within their collection".

The teapots in this book were found at auctions, estate sales, antiques shops, bring and buy sales, flea markets, secondhand shops, and church fairs. Every teapot you purchase for a few pounds will not automatically be worth five to ten times more. Collect for aesthetic and sentimental value rather than for monetary gain. Leave that business to dealers.

Part of the lure in collecting is that every once in a while you will find that buried treasure of a teapot, and will walk away with your purchase knowing you found something really special for a bargain price.

This book is intended as a reference guide rather than a price guide. Prices vary greatly from country to country and even within a country. Across the United States, for example, prices vary through the Mid-States and South. As you would expect, teapots in excellent condition demand higher prices than those with flaws.

The mark on a teapot may be the most important detail in identifying the manufacturer and age. Whether or not a teapot bears a mark, usually on the bottom, should not be the sole factor in the decision to buy. Some teapots can be identified without a mark. In this book a mark is included, where possible, with the caption descriptions of the teapots. As you continue to collect and research your teapots, you will begin to get a feel for age and style. This will help you to determine if an unmarked teapot is made in England or Japan, for example. Study the photos in this book as a learning tool.

Put the kettle on, and reach for your favourite brewing pot. Then settle back to enjoy these pages filled with information and photos of charming teapots.

A Brief History of Teapots

CHAPTER

Chinese Teapots

Tea was first brewed and sipped from cup-like bowls similar to the cups used in Chinese restaurants today. The exact origins of the teapot are unknown, but there are two theories. One is that the teapot evolved from the Islamic coffeepot; the other that the teapot was a modified form of early Chinese wine vessels.

Actually, it may have been a combination of both, considering that the Islamic countries border China. Slowly, the enjoyment of drinking tea spread across the Continent of Asia, reaching coffee-drinking people. Before the first teapots were designed in the 17th century, similar coffeepots and wine vessels were being used. They had short spouts near the top of the body, pointing upward. Designers fashioned handles opposite the spout for ease in pouring. But they also found tea brewed better in uniform, round-bodied pots. These pots still had short spouts similar to the coffeepots or wine vessels they imitated.

Potters continued to refine the shape of teapots, working toward the design best suited to brewing tea. The earliest teapots were approximately the size of the small cups originally used for making and drinking tea. Initially, these teapots were made of red or brown stoneware in the Chinese province of Yixing in southeast China. These first teapots were tiny, not because tea was expensive, for it was grown in China and was readily available, but because each person could have a pot. This produced a headier brew for the individual.

ABOVE LEFT ***Hu-Kwa Tea tin*** **from a long-established importer and marketing company, Mark T. Wendell, in Boston, U.S.A. This tin holds 1 lb/0.45 kg of a tea that is still sold. It dates from the 1950s. The back of the tin reads: "Hu-Kwa Tea, this fine China tea is of distinctive character. To be appreciated it must be made according to these directions: Use freshly boiled water. When the water is boiling hard (so that steam comes out of the nozzle of the kettle furiously) scald out the teapot and put in one generous teaspoon of tea for each person and one 'for the pot'. Pour on the water and allow the tea to draw five and one-half minutes; stir, and let settle say one-half minute. Then decant". The opposite side depicts flowers and reeds.**

The Chinese had great respect for their natural surroundings, a fact that is depicted in everything from architecture to common utensils. Therefore, it is not surprising that the Chinese fashioned delicate teapots into the shape of fruits, animals, bamboo, and tree branches. Such teapots are made to this day.

The Chinese continued to expand their tea production, and exportation grew. Wooden crates were used to transport the tea. Small stoneware teapots and, later, other tea wares, were easily packed inside crates of tea. It is uncertain whether this was a requested bonus by the importers or an incentive to purchase more tea from Chinese traders. By the mid- to late-eighteenth century, the East India Trading Company's sales agents were giving specifications to the Chinese on how to decorate teapots and tea wares, such as cups or bowls, that were packed inside crates of tea.

European potters tried to copy the fine Chinese stoneware teapots, but it would be many years before a durable porcelain was made in England. Chinese teapots symbolize the drinking of tea, and are still imported around the world.

Japanese Teapots

When teapots were introduced to Japan, most likely via Korea during the 9th century, many successful pottery centres had already been established. In fact, the most famous of production centres had been established by Korean immigrants. Tea drinking became a ritualistic ceremony in Japan, beginning with the poor Zen Buddhists and then spreading to the wealthier classes. Tea rooms, buildings exclusively for tea ceremonies, became popular. These were called *Sukiya*, meaning "Abode of Fancy". The Japanese regarded tea-drinking highly, and were therefore very particular about their teapots. Accomplished students of Zen Buddhism were groomed and trained for the art of becoming a Tea Master, and they took a personal interest in how teapots were made.

Porcelain was made in Japan after 1600 in the province of Arita. Porcelain teapots were a mixture of Chinese and Korean designs. A unique characteristic of Japanese teapots is that they were decorated with items found in nature, but they used colours other than

ABOVE ***Gladiator Tea* *advertising card*** **showing a Japanese tea garden at a plantation where Gladiator Tea was grown. Japanese ladies are picking "early in the season, when the leaves are tender and sweet". The date is incomplete, but the postcard was printed at the turn of the century.**

ABOVE ***Boat on the water scene*** **features beautiful hand-painting and a lot of detail all over its body. There is a matching milk jug and sugar bowl. Moriage-style slip is applied on the leaves. The pot is marked "Japan", and was made c.1940.**

those naturally existing. Examples are red trees, orange birds, or a green sky. Soon, English potters were

before the tables turned and Japanese potters began mimicking European teapots, especially those made for export. Teapots and other utensils were created exclusively for the Japanese tea ceremony, and were not intended for exportation.

Japan's unique culture has developed and strengthened over centuries. The field of pottery, porcelain, and china has always been an important part of this culture. The Japanese continue to produce exquisite art pottery, collectible china, and inexpensive novelty items. Teapots made in Japan are widely available in all these forms, and will enhance any collection.

European Teapots

In the late 17th century it was the dream of every European potter to invent a form of pottery as durable as the imported Chinese red and brown stoneware. The Dutch were producing Delftware, but this tin-glazed earthenware proved too delicate to withstand the boiling hot water used for making tea.

In 1709 a German chemist, Johann Friedrich Bottger, discovered a method of producing porcelain that looked like Chinese porcelain. He founded the

How Salt Glaze Teapots were Made

In the early 18th century, while searching for a method to imitate Chinese porcelain, European potters made a discovery. Fine clay and ground flint fired at very high temperatures, with the addition of salt, would produce a hard and durable ware.

During the firing process, heated salt was added to the kiln. It vaporized, and reacted with the silica in the clay to form a thick glaze on the surface. Salt-glazed stoneware teapots could withstand the rigours of boiling water to brew tea every day.

The finest salt-glazed teapots were produced between 1720 and 1740, but the method continued into the next century. Salt-glazed wares gave the Europeans a definite edge over the Chinese imports of that day. Salt glazing lent itself to highly decorative forms, and soon potters were applying enamelled ornamentation.

One way to recognize salt glaze is by the slightly pitted surface, similar to an orange peel, that is left by the process. Salt glaze was replaced by porcelain as the porcelain process spread and was refined. Salt-glazed teapots are rare, and most are found in museums.

ABOVE ***Scalloped green teapot*** **made of a transparent china with fine details on the handle, upper rim, and footed bottom. The flowers are transferred, and the remaining decoration is hand painted. The pot is marked "Germany, Royal Hanover". This pot was made in the late 1920s. A matching sugar bowl and milk jug were also made.**

Meissen factory in 1710, and began making teapots and dinnerware for the royal family. By 1713, Meissen were producing for the open market.

Before this discovery only a soft-paste porcelain was made. The only known way to achieve a certain hardness was to add a glass compound to the clay, and then fire it at low temperatures. But there were difficulties with this procedure, and often pieces lost their shape if not fired precisely.

In the production of porcelain, sometimes called hard-paste, the clay mixture could be fired at high temperatures, resulting in a strong finished product. This discovery revolutionized the industry. The teapot became much more durable, especially for everyday use. Because potters often worked at one factory for a while and then moved on to another company, the "secret process" did not remain a secret for long. Other factories began producing similar teapots.

English Teapots

In the mid-17th century, coffee houses were flourishing in England, but tea quickly became popular, particularly with the wealthy and the aristocrat. Teapots grew in popularity and form in the 18th century. In 1754, Staffordshire potter Josiah Wedgwood formed a partnership with master potter Thomas Whieldon. Wedgwood introduced new ceramic bodies and glazes into the products, and in 1759 he set up his own works in Burslem. Wedgwood are still leaders in the fine china and porcelain world of today.

ABOVE ***Old Worcester – A First Period teapot*, made between 1765 and 1770, and decorated with the Old Japan Star pattern. Note the tilted finial.**

Because the earliest teapots used in England were from China, English potters naturally produced teapots with similar shapes and designs. Potteries sprang up in Plymouth and Bristol, as well as Staffordshire. They all owed much of their success to the fashion for drinking tea and the consequent need for teapots.

Thomas Whieldon also hired and trained a young man named Josiah Spode. After learning the trade, Spode began his own factory, and in 1800 was credited with the invention of bone china. Bone china is made when bone ash reacts with clay, flint, and feldspar to produce a particularly fine, translucent china.

RIGHT **An advertising card from The Great Atlantic & Pacific Tea Company ("A & P"). This beautifully illustrated card, copyrighted 1883, is a forerunner to the business card of today. The illustration shows a Victorian lady having tea – she is sipping her tea from a cup plate of that era. The back of the card has an offer you are invited to pick up at an A & P store, saying ". . . whose name has become a by-word in every household where pure teas and coffees are appreciated".**

In the 19th century, teapots were decorated in varying finishes, such as lustreware, transfer printing, and ornate moulding. Lustreware used a type of glaze with a metal base so that the teapot took on the appearance of a metal pot. Transfer printing was a novel way to decorate with poetry, sayings, and scenery. Ornate moulding included footed teapots, scrollwork, and intricate baroque borders.

Figural teapots – those shaped like people, animals, cottages, or fruit and vegetables – have been produced almost since the conception of teapots. Their popularity has ebbed and flowed through the centuries. Between 1750 and 1800 many figural shapes were produced, then tastes changed to embrace mostly globular and oval shapes. Some early classic 19th-century shapes were New Oval, London, and Rococo.

By the late 19th century, the Arts and Crafts Movement had swung the pendulum in the direction of individual handiwork, and many English factories employed artists who designed and handpainted their wares, including teapots. Clarice Cliff and Susie Cooper are two of the more recognizable English artists employed at this time.

At this same time, figural teapots once again grew in popularity. Caricatures of political figures abounded. Teapots shaped like Toby figures, and tributes to famous people, such as the writer Oscar Wilde and the painter James Whistler, are other examples. From the late 19th century until the present day, English companies have produced figural teapots in every shape imaginable. Well-known factories include Allerton's, Carlton, Gibson's, Lingard, Minton, Price, Royal Worcester, Sadler, Wade, Wedgwood, Wood & Sons, and H. J. Wood.

New World Teapots

The New World that had been established on the American continent continued to grow and flourish. Immigrants brought a variety of skills and trades with them to set up shop in the New World. Pottery production was one of these crafts, and for about three centuries most of what was produced would be considered folk pottery. Shiploads of pottery and porcelain continued to arrive from England to compete with this industry, and even after the notorious Boston Tea Party in 1773, porcelain importation expanded. Transfer printing had been developed, and Wedgwood and other potters sent scouts to bring back scenes that would entice buyers in the New World.

Basically, two types of pottery were produced in the New World. In the New England colonies, earthenware was produced from approximately 1640 to 1785. European immigrants introduced stoneware, which was made from 1700 to early this century.

In the search for the right combination of clays and feldspars, one pottery area that became well known was Bennington, Vermont. Soon potteries opened in New York, New Jersey, and Virginia. In Baltimore, Maryland, an English immigrant first produced the famous "Rebekah at the Well" teapot around 1850.

At about the same time, settlers were moving steadily west. The discovery of clay beds in the Ohio Valley provided the impetus for many pottery companies, some of which still produce teapots and other items. Potteries were often sold or taken over by other potteries in times of financial hardship. All these potteries produced teapots unless the company specialized in tiles or some other industrial ceramic.

The late 19th and early 20th centuries saw a rapid rise in pottery and porcelain manufacturing in America. Most items were made of a heavy pottery, and glazes tended to be thick, but chemists and artists continued to refine their formulas, giving us some lovely teapots to collect.

The difficult thing about collecting teapots from this era is that pottery and porcelain companies did not always mark their wares. Then again, sometimes the glaze would fill in the impressed mark on the bottom of a teapot, making it difficult to see.

ABOVE ***Pyrex etched teapot*** **was made in the late 1930s to early 1940s. Although it appears fragile, it can withstand the heat of boiling water to make tea. The pot has a pretty spray of flowers etched on both sides. The lid has a raised marking, which reads "Corning Pyrex, Made in U.S.A.".**

One company that has stood the test of time is the Hall China Company of East Liverpool, Ohio. Founded in 1903 by Robert Hall, it still produces teapots. While there is not room in this book to mention the many other successful teapot-producing companies (see Further Reading), Hall China is especially noteworthy for their continuous line of teapots. Robert Hall experimented with non-lead glazes and the firing process in an attempt to imitate Chinese porcelain. He succeeded in 1911 with a method that produced a strong, white porcelain with a durable glaze that could be manufactured in one firing. Early wares, including teapots, were made for institutional use, such as in restaurants and hospitals, or on trains. But, in 1930, Hall marketed three teapot shapes for store promotion. Hall China has continued to make teapots to this day. Other American pottery and porcelain companies have also made teapots in a wide variety of shapes and forms. In the early 20th century, Victorian styles were popular. Trends were changing to more modern looks by the Art Deco period beginning around 1925. This meant sleek-looking teapots in pink, black, or gray. Silver and pewter also reflected smoother shapes with less detail and a more aerodynamic look.

In the 1930s, figural teapots gained popularity again, especially those in the form of animals. The Erphila importing company of Philadelphia imported many examples of dogs, cats, and other animal teapots from countries such as Germany and Czechoslovakia.

Commonly found teapots are those made in the U.S. from 1920 to the present. Examples range from heavy pottery and durable porcelain to fine china. In the following pages there are teapots from around the world, giving you ideas of what to look for when collecting.

How to Brew Tea

1. To make the best-tasting tea, you will need a kettle in which to boil water, and a teapot in which to brew the tea.

2. Fill a kettle with fresh water of any temperature, and put it on to boil. Do not reboil water, as the air has been boiled out and the water will be flat.

3. While the water in the kettle is heating, fill your teapot with hot water to preheat the pot. This will help keep the water hot for a longer period of time when added from the kettle for brewing tea. When the water in the kettle begins to boil, pour the water out of the teapot.

4. Add your favourite tea to the teapot. If you are using loose tea, add one teaspoon for each cup and another for the pot. If you are using teabags, keep in mind that most teabags will make two cups, so add bags according to the number of cups your pot holds. For example, a standard six-cup pot would take three teabags. If you like your tea very strong, add another teabag.

5. Bring the teapot to the kettle so the water will be boiling when added to the pot. Place the lid on the teapot, and steep from three to five minutes. Teabags brew much more quickly than loose tea, so two minutes may be long enough if you prefer a lighter tea.

6. Pour out the tea, and add sugar, lemon, or milk as desired. Low-calorie sweeteners also work well in tea, but try sparingly until you find the right taste. Pour tea made with loose leaves through a strainer.

7. Refill the pot from the kettle for more cups of tea. Remove teabags or loose tea after the second brewing; do not leave the leaves in the pot, or the tea may become too strong and bitter.

8. After refilling the teapot, you may want to use a tea cosy to keep the tea hot for second and third cups.

LEFT ***A most colourful postcard*** **illustrates "The Bachelor's Meal," with his teapot and large teacup nearby. The card is not dated, but it only required a one (U.S.) cent stamp to mail.**

FIGURAL TEAPOTS

CHAPTER 2

Not long after the invention of the teapot, designers began moulding it into characteristic shapes. While the round-bodied teapot has proved to be the best for brewing tea and most often pours without dripping, imaginations have never left teapots alone. Although the whimsy of figural teapots has kept them collectible for centuries, they have less frequently found their way to the tea table compared with their bulbous counterparts in china, porcelain, or pottery.

This chapter is divided into five categories of teapot shapes that are all called "Figural." Included are cottages and houses, animals, people, food, and objects.

Pouring without sputtering or dripping is a problem with many of these figural teapots. If you intend to use your figural teapot for tea, it is wise to consider the shape and placement of the spout. To pour properly, the spout should have a curved opening and extend beyond the body of the teapot. The curve of the opening will determine how well the tea will pour and if it will drip. The more elongated the spout opening, the less likely it will be to drip. If the spout is a mere hole somewhere on the side of the formed body, it may sputter, and pouring may be disappointing. If you collect figural teapots for aesthetic pleasure, this need not be a worry.

The first figural teapots were made in the 17th century by potters in the Chinese province of Yixing near Shanghai in southeast China. Yixing pots had forms like a lotus flower, a small melon or a pear, or partially depicted a dragon. Similar pots are still made today in smooth, natural clay, which develops a rich patina with use. In fact, it is recommended that these pots not be washed, but rinsed with cool water. The residual build-up from brewing tea "seasons" the teapot, and enhances the tea's flavour.

ABOVE LEFT ***Gray dragon teapot with cup and saucer.*** **This style is often called moriage ware. Moriage is a Japanese decoration of slipwork applied in relief. Dragon ware is still made today, so collectors need to study this field. Newer pieces lack detail, and not as much slip is applied. This set was purchased in 1924 at Garfinkel's Department Store in Washington, D.C. It is marked with "Japan" and a garland, which includes the letter "T".**

ABOVE ***Wide-mouthed snail*** **A brightly glazed teapot made in Japan in the 1970s. It was made in other colours such as red. It has an impressed mark.**

Two importers in the U.S. specialize in Yixing teapots, although they may be found in quality import shops around the U.S. One such company, The World Treasure Trading Company, offers a particular assortment of Yixing teapots (see Useful Addresses). This importer, in agreement with Chinese tea aficionados, regards Yixing teapots as the best vessel for brewing tea. The wares they offer are sought after by collectors as well. Shapes impart an elegant simplicity, with themes from nature or the animal kingdom.

Margaret Chung is an importer and purveyor of fine-quality teas and Yixing teapots from China and Taiwan. She and her husband operate Madame Chung Finest Teas, Inc. with hands-on experience from their homeland of China. While living in China, Yixing teapots were a common household item for them, along with the Gongfu method of brewing tea (see Box). Then they came to America, their stock of tea ran out, and they found it difficult to obtain quality Chinese tea in the U.S. At the same time, Margaret was using the subject of Chinese tea and teawares for a course at the University of Chicago. The combination of a practical need and researching the subject brought them to begin their import company, specializing in Gongfu tea.

The modern Yixing teapots offered through Madame Chung Finest Teas are modelled after originals, including a melon, a lotus flower, a dragon, a gourd, an egg, and a pear. Some more modernistic shapes are the square-round, a version of the cube teapot; a triangular shape, with three circles for a handle; and the ewer teapot, which takes its design from the wine ewer. A Gongfu set includes two tiny, round-bodied teapots.

THE GONGFU TEA TRADITION

The Chinese word Gongfu (Kung-fu) does not simply refer to the martial arts discipline that we know. It includes many activities that require time, patience, and effort to master. It is a 1,000-year-old tradition of brewing and drinking tea that is not only enjoyable but entertaining as well.

The basic Gongfu set includes two tiny, Yixing teapots (or sometimes a teapot and a tea jug), a tea bowl, and six teacups. It is also helpful to add a set of bamboo tea accessories, which include a scoop, tongs, and a scraper in a holder; these are for handling, measuring, and removing tea during this process. A tray on which to place all items, and a timer, will add convenience.

When making tea the Gongfu way, after heating water to boiling, the teapot is rinsed with hot water, then the water is poured into the bowl and the teapot filled about one-third with loose tea leaves handled with the scoop. The tea leaves are given a rinse by filling the pot half-full with hot water, then draining the water out immediately, leaving only the soaked tea leaves.

Now fill the pot to the top with more hot water, cover, and pour additional water over the teapot resting in the tea bowl. Now the tea cups are warmed with a rinse of hot water. The tea should be steeped for only 30 seconds. After steeping, pour the tea into the second teapot or tea jug and serve. More water can be added to the teapot, and up to five infusions can be made from the same tea leaves; add 10 more seconds for the second brewing, and 15 additional seconds thereafter.

With the miniature Yixing teapots, the bouquet and flavour of tea by the Gongfu method is savoured in much the same manner as a vintage wine. Many types of Chinese tea are excellent for the Gongfu method, including black, green, Oolong (semi-fermented), and scented teas such as jasmine and Pu Erh (Poor-err), which is grown only in a certain area of China and is low in caffeine.

TYPES OF TEA AND PROCESSING

Tea is made from the leaves of the plant *Camellia sinensis*, which is an evergreen bush. It has two subspecies: *sinensis* (small leaf) and *assamica* (large leaf). The tea is first classified by their colour and quality, then processed.

ABOVE ***Advertising postcard*** **This beautifully illustrated card shows young ladies from India and reads on the front, "From the Orient – Whence come the fragrant India and Ceylon Tea." It advises how much tea to use to get the best results. This postcard is dated 1907 and stamped "For Sale By: Union Gro. Co., Hillsboro, Ohio".**

BLACK TEA is a fully fermented tea. It is picked from young leaves. Its discovery was an accident: in the late 1600s, a load of semi-fermented tea on its way to Britain was delayed and became fully fermented. Upon its arrival, the new taste was enjoyed and became popular.

GREEN TEA is most popular among Orientals, and has more variations and stimulants than other types of teas. It is not fermented, is green in colour, and the true taste of each variety can only be found in brewing.

OOLONG is a semi-fermented tea, picked from mature leaves. It has a fruity flavour with a lingering fragrance. Oolong grown in Taiwan has become the most popular tea world-wide.

SCENTED OR FLAVOURED TEAS are made by using either Black or Oolong tea and adding natural oils for flavouring, or spices and dried flowers or fruit. Jasmine is the most popular flavoured Chinese tea but others have caught on in recent years, such as cinnamon, lemon, mango, and other tropical fruits, almond, mint, and orange.

Specialty shops have sprung up across the U.S.; try looking in your *Yellow Pages* under "Tea" or "Coffee". Fine tea can also be mail-ordered, but you may want to request a company's brochure before ordering (see Useful Addresses).

COTTAGES AND HOUSES

Salt-glazed teapots in the form of houses were made as early as 1750 by Staffordshire potters. Chinese potters before this era had fashioned delicate teapots shaped like houses, but they resembled pagodas or other Oriental buildings, with roofs curving upward.

While cottage and house teapots were generically designed, many others depicted a famous house or castle. Japanese house teapots more often were styled after the tea house. An interesting mix of styles is presented by the Staffordshire house teapot, which has a decidedly Eastern serpent or dragon's head as the spout.

Cottage and house teapots have been produced continually through the centuries, some shaped very practically for tea time and others as mere souvenirs or

ABOVE ***Village Tea Room*** **was made by Lenox as a part of a collectible series of Victorian houses. The mark on the bottom reads, "The Lenox Village Tea Room, Fine Porcelain, dated 1991, made in Taiwan".**

ABOVE ***Large cottage*** Cottage ware is a popular theme in teapots and English country cottages are especially popular. This larger cottage is impressed on its bottom with "Ye Olde Cottage" and "Made in England". It was made by Price Kensington. It is also marked with a wreath. Other matching pieces were made c.1930.

ABOVE ***Country cottage set*** made before 1945. Colourful details are handpainted under the glaze, and all pieces are marked "Made in Japan". The teapot is 5½ in/14 cm high.

whimsical objects. Cottage ware has become a collectible category in its own right, and collectors seek all types of ware shaped like country or English cottages. Price Brothers of England has been a big producer of cottage ware, but in close competition is Japanese cottage ware.

Modern versions of cottage and house teapots are being produced even today. A large cottage with a chimneyed roof as the lid was produced by Price Kensington in England, reading "Ye Olde Cottage." This same shape and similar colour cottage teapot was reproduced in the 1980s, but beware of reproductions made to look like older wares. Highly regarded by collectors, cottage and house teapots made in England or marked "Made in Occupied Japan" command slightly higher prices than those simply marked "Japan." Other teapots in this category are shaped like windmills, watermills, country stores, castles, or even teepees. The largest cottage teapot – a renovated quick-stop store – is located in Chester, West Virginia. Dubbed "The World's Largest Teapot," it is 12 feet high and 44 feet in circumference, with a handle that is 10 feet tall; windows adorn the body. Cottages and houses have been such a part of human life that it seems natural for teapots to be fashioned after our places of dwelling.

Modern ceramicists have elaborated on the theme of cottages and houses by creating teapots shaped like a 1950s roadside diner, industrial buildings, or skyscrapers. But when putting the kettle on for tea time, the English cottage with a thatched roof will more often be the choice.

ABOVE ***Two cottages*** made in the mid-1970s in Japan. There is handpainted detail under the glaze on both. The round hut is not marked, but the square cottage is marked with a label and "Marketed by Bradshaw Int'l of California".

ANIMALS

People have always had an affinity for animals, which is evident in the number of teapots depicting them. Through the ages, books and artwork have continually portrayed people with their pets nearby or their herds in the field. History tells us that people have hunted, ridden, coralled, and domesticated animals. But what about on the tea table?

The majority of animal teapots have not been designed with tea-making in mind, but they have remained popular. Most animal-shaped teapots are items of novelty, and conversation pieces more than items used to brew a cup of tea. The novelty of animal-shaped teapots has inspired stories and poems that combine teatime and favourite animals, such as the one that follows:

LEFT ***Blue bird*** **is a teapot with a cheery smile. It was made in Japan. It holds about three cups and is 7 × 7 in/17.5 × 17.5 cm.**

ABOVE ***Hitchhiking frog atop a duck*** **is an unmarked teapot that was either an individual ceramicist's project, or was made in Japan. The frog adds some whimsy to this serious-looking duck.**

PUSSY TO TEA

Old English Rhyme, author unknown

"Pussy cat, pussy cat,
Where are you at?
Where are your manners,
You bad little cat?"
"Miou," said the pussy;
"Please, may I stay
To afternoon tea, ma'am,
For once, just this day?"

"Pussy cat, pussy cat,
What can I do?
There's no cup and saucer,
There's no tea for you."

"Miou," said the pussy;
"Miou, ma'am," said she.
"I don't need a teacup,
I never take tea;
Some milk in a saucer
Is better for me."

RIGHT ***Beckoning cat*** **This is a favourite figural among animal teapot collectors. The paper label reads "Cortendorf, West Germany" and the pot is stamped with the same on the bottom. The pot is 9 in/23 cm high and 9½ in/24 cm from spout to tail.**

With their popularity as pets, it is no wonder that cats are also a favourite theme for figural teapots. And the beckoning cat pose is the most popular, possibly because of this old story:

THE TEMPLE CAT

In a small Asian village was a temple located high upon a hill. It was falling into ruin because the village was poor, and few people bothered to climb the hill to visit and support the temple. The priests were even considering closing it down.

One day a curious tourist climbed the hill to see the temple, and, as he passed by a window, he spied a cat perched on the sill. The cat sat with its paw extended, beckoning the tourist. It was almost as if the cat were waving for him to come in. The traveller was so touched by the beckoning of the cat that when he returned to the village he told everyone about the cat and encouraged them to go and see it.

As word spread, more and more people began to visit the temple, which prospered. With the return of so many visitors, restoration began. And all because of the beckoning cat.

Cat teapots are also made in many other poses, such as two cats dancing, an aproned cat – herself the teapot – ready to serve tea, and a pair of kittens dressed as bride and groom.

Black cat teapots continued to be another favourite of collectors. They were made from the 1920s to the present in various shapes and sizes. A nested tea cosy was also made in Japan. The eyes, whiskers, ears, or other highlights on black cats from about 1920 to the early 1950s were handpainted over the glaze. This painted detail often rubbed or washed off, making those examples with most of their paint intact more desirable to collectors. A cat collectors club has been formed for enthusiasts of feline-shaped items, including teapots (see Useful Addresses).

Cats are not the only animal-shaped teapots receiving attention. Almost any imaginable animal has been portrayed in a teapot. Domesticated pets are favourites, but bizarre examples can be found, such as the 20th-century creation of a silver-plated tea set in the shape of flies.

LEFT ***Demure beckoning cat*** **A pot with no mark, made by an individual artist. It features handpainted detail under the glaze.**

RIGHT ***Begging cockapoo*** **has a satin finish with whimsical detail. It was made in Japan c.1960s, and marketed by Lefton's. It has a paper label on the bottom.**

RIGHT ***Dancing kitties*** **This example is one of a series of dancing teapots marketed by Applause, Inc. of Woodland Hills, California, and made in Korea. This teapot was made in the 1980s and is still sold in finer gift shops. It is not very practical for pouring tea as the spout sputters and drips, but it makes a wonderful addition to any collection.**

BELOW RIGHT ***Fish for lunch*** **This small teapot of a common design was made and marked in China. This teapot is only 5¼ in/13.3 cm high. Other versions, with or without fish, were made in Taiwan. There are also imitations of Satsuma beckoning cat teapots.**

Second in popularity to cat teapots are figurals of dogs. The majority of dog teapots are made in the begging position, with front paws raised. To fit the shape of a teapot, many other animals are depicted in this same stance, such as rabbits or bears. Others have front paws raised and holding some object. Examples are a squirrel holding a nut, a mouse holding cheese, or a panda holding sugar cane. The trunk of an elephant lends itself naturally as a spout, while the large body provides an admirably rounded pot. Elephant teapots have often been made by Oriental manufacturers.

Whatever animal figure is currently in vogue, collectors will find in a teapot. In the early 1990s, when cows were popular, various cow teapots were produced by English and Japanese manufacturers.

Within the figural category, more animal-shaped teapots have been made than any other genre. Collectors hunt for animals not yet part of their teapot zoo, such as a frog, an alligator, a monkey, or a bird. In the last 50 years, manufacturers have looked to animal cartoon characters, which are always popular among collectors. Examples in this area are Mickey Mouse and Donald Duck. Animal figural teapots are a category that continues to expand, and collectors do not have to worry about a narrow market.

RIGHT ***Elephants for tea time*** **An especially popular animal figure because the trunk forms a natural spout. The large teapot has a *mahmout* – elephant guide – sitting in a howdah, a seat for a rider. It is marked on the bottom of a foot "Made in Japan" and "Chungai", (a province in Japan). It was made c.1940. The small elephant, with another elephant in the howdah, is a newer creation and can be found in import shops. It is marked "Made in China" on the bottom, along with Chinese characters.**

ABOVE ***Blue and white rooster*** **marked "Made in China". It has been made from the late 1980s. This example is only 3½ in/9 cm high, but other shapes and sizes of this blue and white china are widely imported.**

ABOVE ***Cow-in-boots*** **– but why this cow needs boots is not clear. This teapot is a recent creation of Fiona Stokes, marketed by Otagiri of Japan, inspired by the current popularity of cows.**

ABOVE ***Japanese duo*** **The bodies of these teapots were made c.1948 from one mould; only the heads differ. They are marked "Made in Japan". This novelty ware has been made in quantity and was sold primarily in chain stores.**

ABOVE ***Wide-eyed owl*** **This teapot, made c.1960, has "Japan" impressed on the bottom. Several matching pieces were made, such as salt and pepper shakers.**

ABOVE ***Squirrel's tea for two*** **The shape of an acorn is turned into a teapot housing three mischievous squirrels. It was made c.1977 in Japan, and carries a paper label reading Enesco, along with an impressed "M. R." A nested cosy, milk jug and sugar bowl are also available.**

ABOVE ***White dragon*** **features a raised relief of a dragon on the body, and coralene detail. It was made c.1940. It is marked "D M" in a triangle, and "Made in Japan". Tea sets are available. Some have lithopane cups with an impression of a geisha in the bottom, which is revealed when the cup is held up to the light.**

People

The earliest examples of teapots in the shape of human forms are those of Chinese people, or rather the Chinese God of Plenty. They are often holding an object, such as a parrot, a snake, or some fruit. The earliest such pots date from *c.* 1748 and reside in museums. The late 19th century brought a renewed interest in teapots shaped like human figures, again with Chinese figures doing things such as lugging a heavy bundle or holding fruit.

This was the era for Toby teapots. Toby jugs, and therefore teapots, were named after Toby Philpots, the character in the song "The Little Brown Jug." At first the figure depicted only various versions of this fictional character, but then a trend began for moulding famous people into Toby-type figures. One such example, which was made over a long period of time, is a teapot showing a three-legged man sitting on a stump, as a souvenir from the Isle of Man. Two legs straddle the stump while another appears to be kicking backwards, but is actually the spout. One of the most well-known figures is a teapot portraying the writer Oscar Wilde. On one side is the face of a man and on the reverse is a woman. Inscribed on the bottom is "Fearful consequences through the laws of Natural Selection and Evolution of living up to one's teapot".

With modern pottery and porcelain techniques, shaping a teapot after well-known personages has continued. In recent times, the bust of Ronald Reagan has been fashioned both by the Hall China Co. of the U.S., and Carlton Ware in England. A whole series of

RIGHT ***Father and child*** **is an unmarked teapot made of fine white porcelain, possibly made in China, c.1970.**

LEFT ***Ronald Reagan*** **Made in the late 1980s as a caricature of the former U.S. President, this teapot turns collectors' heads. It was commissioned by an English gentleman, who could not be located after the pot was produced. Fortunately, the American manufacturers Hall China had no problem in selling it.**

Charles Dickens characters has been produced. The cartoon character Andy Capp is portrayed in a wonderful teapot by Wade of England. Swineside Ceramics, also of England, markets an amazing line of figural teapots of people engaged in common activities and some wild looking people, too. Examples include a punk rocker with a Mohican hairstyle, a trumpet player, a bellhop, a vampire, and a geisha girl. Much sought after is a teapot fashioned after the Mad Hatter by Tony Wood Ltd.; this teapot was marketed by the British Tea Council. But where is the teapot of Alice and the March Hare? You will find all three *Alice in Wonderland* characters moulded on a teapot with a heart handle and a spade spout called Mad Hatter's Tea Party, which is available through the Collector's Teapot.

ABOVE ***Snow White*** **with four of the seven dwarfs marching along her dress to the tune of "Hi Ho, Hi Ho". The pot was made in Japan, but is marked "Walt Disney Productions". A musical box underneath plays the infamous tune. This pot was made in the late 1940s.**

Walt Disney characters have always been a favourite of collectors, and many teapots have been made from the 1940s to the present. A Snow White musical teapot with some of the dwarfs in relief is a charming example. Currently on the market is a rather large musical teapot of the *Beauty and the Beast* character Mrs. Potts. A Mrs. Potts teapot cookie jar is also available, along with other accessories such as a cup named Chip. In 1989, Disney was marketing a set of Mickey and Minnie Mouse four-cup teapots in a lovely glossy black with finely painted details. Accessories included a matching Mickey and Minnie milk jug and sugar bowl, and salt and pepper shakers. The Disney Store is a chain that has sprung up across the U.S. in major shopping malls, but they also have a mail order catalogue (see Useful Addresses).

The well-known sleuth Sherlock Holmes has been turned into a large teapot. This teapot, manufactured by Hall China, now with its matching mug, was the inspiration of Dan Brasier and his wife, Ann. The idea was a merger of their two favourite interests: Sherlock Holmes and collecting Hall China. The approaching Centennial Celebration of the first Sherlock Holmes novel was the impetus they needed to get their idea off the ground.

Dan contacted Hall China to find out how they handled an idea from an individual, knowing the

ABOVE ***Mrs. Potts and Chip*** **both play the theme song from *Beauty and the Beast*. Both are marked "Beauty and the Beast, handpainted, The Walt Disney Company". They have been made in Malaysia since 1991 and are marketed by Schmid. Mrs Potts is 7 in/18 cm high, Chip 4½ in/11 cm.**

company mainly deals with commercial china production. Hall China were very friendly, and Dan was put in touch with their Design Studio Head, Don Schreckengost. He was willing to take on the idea of a Sherlock Holmes teapot, and personally did all of the design and modelling work – the backstamp on the pot has Dan's and Don's initials respectively. The making of this teapot entailed seven case moulds, or 14 separate pieces. The first 500 teapots to be sold are numbered, setting them apart from later production.

In collecting figural teapots shaped like people, one could easily fill a room with all types of characters. The shape of a teapot lends itself well to a body, head, arms, and sometimes even legs.

RIGHT ***Sherlock Holmes teapot*** **This pot was individually commissioned by Dan Brasier and fashioned by Don Schreckengost of Hall China. It was made c.1988 and is marked on the bottom. It is 12 in/30 cm high and just over 12 in/30 cm from the pipe spout to the handle. It is a little too heavy for pouring tea, but is a definite conversation piece. Mugs are available.**

BELOW ***Maid teapot*** **was made in the 1970s and is marked "Eda, Mann, an Eda Original", with a sticker that says "Mann, Japan".**

ABOVE ***Scotty teapot*** **is fashioned after the English cartoon character Andy Capp. It was made by Wade of England between 1953 and 1955. All detail is handpainted. Four variations in the colour of his cap were made.**

ABOVE ***Lady with a hat*** **– her lid. The paper label is still intact, and reads "Handpainted Coronet, Japan". This c.1950 teapot is a charmer on the tea table. Other matching pieces were made.**

ABOVE ***Friar Tuck*** **with crossed eyes is a cute little man made in Japan, but the teapot is unmarked. It was an obvious attempt to copy the renowned Goebel Friar Tuck series. Other matching pieces are available.**

ABOVE ***Mermaid teapot*** **was designed and crafted by an up-and-coming ceramicist, Eliza Hurdle from Bristol, England. It is a light pot, and does not drip, even with this style of spout. It is currently available with matching accessories.**

FOOD

Shaping teapots after various types of food dates back to the early Yixing teapots, and continues to the present. A 1994 mail-order catalogue offered a teapot shaped like a head of cabbage, with a rabbit peeking out of the centre. Matching soup bowls and plates are shaped like a head of cabbage, a bunch of carrots, asparagus spears, an ear of corn, and lettuce leaves.

Fruits and vegetables are the most common shapes, possibly because their naturally round forms are easily adapted to a teapot. Other types of food have also found their way into the teapot genre. One of the most famous is the doughnut shape. The Hall China Company has cornered the market on this eye-catching shape in many different colours. This style has also been made by Chinese and Japanese companies in smaller versions. A similar teapot, reminiscent of Lifesavers, was made by South Western Ceramics for Polo Mints.

Collectors will also find teapots depicting wedding cakes, cherry-topped cupcakes, and loaves of bread. In the early 1980s, a teapot was offered shaped like a fast-food hamburger. The ideas for food-shaped teapots are practically endless, and collectors can expect to find new items offered each year.

OBJECTS

Certain inanimate objects lend themselves to the shape of a teapot quite easily. Others stretch their true shape to fit the teapot mould. Consider the shape of a watering can. At first glance, it is hard to tell that it is a teapot, with the handle and spout in the same proportion and positions as on a teapot. Now consider the shape of a motorcycle; there is no resemblance to a teapot, and even to imagine pouring tea from such an oddly shaped teapot seems bizarre. Both shapes are available from The Collector's Teapot, along with 60 other figural pots.

Teapots shaped like objects have one basic problem: they rarely pour well. Because the spout is formed to fit the object more often than to pour tea gracefully, sputters and drips are common. Handles may also be

ABOVE ***Doughnut*** **This is one of the more common themes of the novelty teapots. This version, made by the U.S. company, Hall China, is in Chinese red, but it is also made in cobalt and delphinium, and there are decorated lines. There is also a matching jug. Doughnut has been made since 1938. Hall China teapots continue to be prized by collectors.**

ABOVE ***Yellow apple*** **There is handpainted detail on this translucent china pot and its matching milk jug. It is unmarked, but possibly Japanese or German manufacture, and dates from c.1930s.**

ABOVE ***An apple a day*** **is the theme of this shiny red teapot. It is unmarked, but is possibly Japanese. It was made c.1950.**

ABOVE ***Trunk and suitcase*** **was designed by Martin Bibby and is currently available, marketed through Swineside Ceramics in England. It is heavy and serviceable, and a conversation piece.**

ABOVE ***A ride through the sun roof*** **This Bubble car teapot was designed by Martin Bibby and sold through Swineside Ceramics in England. Note the license plate, which reads "TEA I".**

ABOVE ***Teatime tunes*** **This piano teapot is a small version of a shape that has recently found its way on to the market in many variations, and makes an inexpensive addition to the figural collection. One of the best examples was designed by Martin Bibby and marketed through Swineside Ceramics in England. This teapot is rather square in shape, made in China, and bears an illegible company name on the bottom.**

awkwardly placed, and lids often slip off. If the teapot body has a busy shape, it may not brew tea evenly, and can be hard to clean on the inside.

There are some designers who have successfully fashioned object teapots to brew and pour for the most discriminating tea enthusiast. One is the Hull Ebb Tide conch-shell-shaped teapot. This not only retains the original shell shape, but is an easily used teapot.

Figural teapots in all categories will continue to grow in popularity; there are many people who do not collect teapots or drink tea, who count a figural teapot or two among their treasures.

ABOVE ***Hull shell teapot*** **is from this U.S. company's Ebb Tide line of ware. Note the seahorse finial. There is a matching milk jug and sugar bowl. This pot is marked "Hull", and was made in the 1950s.**

ABOVE ***Japanese puzzle pot*** **The puzzle is how the tea travels through the pot after brewing through the middle. This pot was found in the corner of a small shop in Okinawa, Japan.**

ABOVE ***Honey in your tea?*** **This beehive teapot was a common country theme from the late 1940s into the 1950s. It was made in Japan.**

CHAPTER 3

FINE CHINA

Producing teapots in fine china has a history dating from the 18th century. The light weight of fine china and the market appeal, even from early production, has made it a highly desirable medium for decorative and practical utensils.

The terms "china" and "porcelain" are often used interchangeably, and for good reason. There are two types of porcelain: hard-paste and soft-paste. Soft-paste porcelain is softer and not as durable. It is fired at lower temperatures than hard-paste, and can be compared to ceramics.

The china referred to in this chapter is the hard-paste porcelain with translucent qualities. Firing temperatures and the mixtures of clay or kaolin with china rock determine whether or not the china will be translucent. A later chapter is devoted to porcelain that is opaque and very durable.

Bone china is a type of hard-paste porcelain developed first by Josiah Spode, but used extensively in England and other countries. It is made by adding bone ash to the china clay and rock. This process produces a very stable medium when fired, and a hard, durable ware. The light weight and translucent qualities of bone china make it very appealing.

ABOVE LEFT ***Willow variant*** **This small London Shape teapot is not decorated with the true Blue Willow design, but with a similar pattern called Spode's Tower. Made in and marked "Copeland, England", it has "Spode" impressed in the porcelain. A complete dinnerware line was made in this pattern, along with a larger-sized teapot. This pot is 4½ in/11.5 cm high, and holds about two cups.**

ABOVE ***Orange lustre teapot*** **in a square shape was made by the Crooksville China Co. of Ohio, which operated between 1902 and 1959.**

ABOVE ***Wedgwood jasperware set*** **Blue and white jasperware has become a symbol of Wedgwood, whose mark, "Wedgwood, Made in England" is stamped on all three pieces. After 1930 Wedgwood items were impressed with the last two numbers of the year of manufacture (56 = 1956). The white bas-relief ornamentation on jasperware traditionally consists of images, scenes, and figures from classical Greek myths, as on these pieces, but other motifs were used.**

Any type of animal bone can be used to create bone china. In *Know Your Antiques*, by Ralph and Terry Kovel, the authors cite an example at the Spode Museum in England where "a punch bowl was made from bones that were left after a banquet. When the guests at the party finished eating, the bones left on plates were collected and burned to ashes." Then they were used in the clay to make the bone china bowl.

ABOVE ***White and floral scallops*** **adorn this pot from Czechoslovakia, which is marked "Epaig, D.F." This pot might be a coffeepot: note that the spout starts closer to the bottom of the pot, and has very little curve. There is no strainer on the inside to keep tea leaves from floating out. This pot is part of a dinner-ware line. It is 8¼ in/21.5 cm high.**

Bone china has been produced in every pottery- and porcelain-producing country, but quality is variable. Collectors can easily find translucent bone china made in Japan that is very crude, with pock marks in the glaze and roughness on unglazed undersides. German and American pieces have been found in the same condition. Depending upon the factory and the skill of workmanship, bone china can be a very fine piece of ware with smooth lines and few, if any, imperfections, or it can be crude and rough. Obviously, the finer pieces are more desirable and demand higher prices.

ABOVE ***Iridescent oval teapot*** **A pot with a locking lid was created in a classic shape that was popular from the late 19th to the early 20th century. Its lovely iridescent glaze has gold details, but shows wear from use as a treasured teapot. It is marked on the bottom with "D & C" in a wreath, and "Made in Poland".**

ABOVE ***Translucent china pot*** **in a dainty oval shape with a locking lid. The floral design is hand-applied transfer. The pot is marked on the bottom with a circled banner and "Victoria, Carlsbad, Austria". It is 5½ in/14 cm high.**

We are most familiar with the fine china of dinnerware sets. Especially notable are the following companies: Haviland, Irish Belleek, Kensington, Lenox, Noritake, Pfaltzgraff, Royal Doulton, and Wedgwood. There are many more companies which through the years have produced translucent but durable china dinnerware. Reference books are available for researching any china dinnerware company. Check your library first, then your local bookshops.

As you collect teapots and get to know various types of ware, you will be able to determine when a teapot may be part of a dinnerware line. It is hard to resist adding pieces that match a certain teapot. In recent years, companies have been established that will search dinnerware lines and find matching pieces. The U.S. company, Kitchen, Etc., has outlets and a mail-order catalogue business specializing in hundreds of dinnerware patterns, including complete sets that often include the teapot and/or milk jug and sugar bowl (see Useful Addresses).

ABOVE ***Individual teapot*** **with an iridescent glaze, made in Czechoslovakia. It is 4 in/10 cm high. Other matching pieces were made.**

Irish Belleek china has caught the attention of collectors for a long time, but this pottery company had many ups and downs before Belleek parian ware was a successful china. The company was founded in the Irish village of Belleek around 1857. It was not until after World War II, however, that factory improvements were made to ensure stable production of parian ware.

ABOVE ***Iridescent-glazed teapot,*** **decorated with modern lines. It is not marked, but once had a paper label. It was possibly made in Poland.**

Parian is a porcelaneous ceramic ware composed mainly of kaolin and feldspar. Two of the founders of the pottery continued to experiment with the porcelain composition until they found the right combination to produce the Belleek parian ware we know today, which is both light and thin. In fact, most Belleek seems too fine for use, but it is nonetheless durable.

The Belleek company produces many different lines, but their Shamrock ware is the one most people are familiar with. Their designs are taken from nature, with handles and finials that resemble twigs, shapes of sea shells, and background patterns like basketweave. Belleek parian china is made today in almost the same way it was originally produced. The workers at the pottery take pride in their work, and live in the village of Belleek or the nearby countryside. If you acquire Irish Belleek, you can be assured that it was crafted with careful hands in a tradition that is almost 150 years old.

LEFT ***Irish Belleek teapot* in a shell and coral motif is about as delicate as the natural items it depicts. It is marked on the bottom with a common Irish Belleek green backstamp. It is 6¾ in/17 cm high.**

RIGHT ***R.S. Prussia teapot* has pearlized lustre finish with surrealistic dogwood blossoms and gold enamelling.**

LEFT ***Meissen teapot and plate* are highly decorated in gold and look too beautiful to use. They were made c.1850.**

ABOVE ***George Washington teapot*** **also features wife Martha on the reverse side. It is not marked, but was possibly by Homer Laughlin. This U.S. company produced a plate and cup with the same decal for the Bicentennial of the birth of George Washington in 1932. The pot holds two cups.**

ABOVE ***American flags and eagle*** **This highly patriotic teapot is unmarked, but its shape, and its wicker handle are characteristic of Japanese teapots. It is 9 in/22.8 cm high.**

Back in the U.S., a pattern that has continued to be popular is that of commemorative items. Any china with the founding father, George Washington, is collectible, along with other patriotic themes, such as eagles or flags. Of course, not all of these items were produced in the U.S. Japanese, European, and English china manufacturers have cashed in on the desirability of patriotic decoration.

The eagle became the United States' national symbol in 1782 after much deliberation. The seal we see today is the seventh die cut since that first design was approved. So, if you find a different seal design on a teapot or a picture, it might help you to date it if you research the national symbol. Soon after the national symbol was decided upon, European potters began sending china to the new country decorated with the American eagle motif.

In a collecting field of their own are British commemorative items. These were mainly produced in Great Britain, but sometimes blanks were used from Germany or Japan and decorated elsewhere. Teapots

RIGHT ***Two souvenir teapots*** **The one-cup pot on the left is decorated with a scene of the U.S. Capitol. It has a quaint square shape with lots of gold decoration. The teapot on the right depicting "Cliffs Near Newport Beach" is 4 in/10 cm high. The scenes on both pots are stencilled designs which were painted on, then hand-painted colour was applied.**

abound that honour British royalty. They are relatively easy to date, often with a date in the design.

Souvenir items are related to commemoratives. Collecting souvenir items has become so popular that collectors now have their own periodical, *Antique Souvenir Collector's News*. The majority of collectible souvenir items are made of fine china from Germany, although Japan has a corner on this market. Older items have handpainted transfer designs of the various places for which they are souvenirs. Some items are dated along with the written description of the visited place, but others are very hard to date. If the souvenir is also for a special event, such as an opening or a dedication, it will be easier to date.

Among the most sought-after souvenir items are china pieces coated with a cobalt glaze. Other small tea sets made in Japan are inexpensive and easily collected. Usually they include a teapot and a cup and saucer, with a display stand. The teapots are also found individually. Collectors in the U.S. face a challenge in collecting only items from one state, or trying to find an example from all 50 states.

LEFT ***Charles and Diana*** **This teapot is one of many commemoratives of this famous couple. These are popular among collectors, disregarding the marital status of their subjects. On the back appear the words "Their Royal Highnesses, The Prince and Princess of Wales". The teapot is not marked. It was made in the 1980s, possibly in Germany as a blank, and then decorated in England.**

ABOVE ***Oriental garden teapot*** **is delicately decorated with applied trees and figures. A paper label on the bottom reads "Ardalt, Japan, Verithin". This transparent china pot could be used for tea, but it is not very practical. It is 8 in/ 20 cm high.**

ABOVE ***Blue willow teapot*** **is made of fine china by Royal Doulton, England. The mark reads "Booth's Real Old Willow". This piece is from Doulton's Majestic line of tableware, and dated 1981.**

RIGHT ***Handpainted flowers*** **This pot is marked with an unusual shade of turquoise, and "Handpainted, Japan", with a circle and two entwined diamonds, and the letters "T T".**

RIGHT ***Noritake teapot*** **is from the Linden pattern of china, which was marketed for many years as a premium item with the Larkin Soap Company during the 1930s. It is highly decorated with applied transfers and handpainting. It is marked "R.C." on the bottom.**

ABOVE ***Violets*** **is a nested cosy set in fine china, with a moulded finial and handpainted detail. It was made in Japan and marketed by Lefton's. Other matching pieces were made.**

LEFT ***Swirled floral teapot*** **is made of transparent china and has lots of handpainted details. The handle of twigs and the small spout are Eastern in style, yet this unmarked teapot was possibly made in Germany.**

ABOVE ***Celadon tea set*** **Celadon is a colour commonly used in Chinese ware. Decoration on this little set with its own tray was done by pressing rice grains into the clay body. When fired, the rice disintegrates, leaving an impression, which the glaze fills in and darkens. This gives a translucent effect, and when cups or teapot are held to the light, it shines through the rice designs. Paper labels on all these pieces say "Made in China".**

China teapots made in China often have their own characteristics, but may be finely detailed or crudely produced. Celadon coloured sets made specifically for export are of higher quality than those found in discount stores. Service people have contributed to the number of teapots and tea sets found in the U.S. Most overseas commissaries will have tea sets made specifically for export. In China, their wares are made for a specific market: either for their own people, or for exportation. When visiting a large city such as Beijing, one would not find the same type of teapot used by the people for sale in the tourist area of the city. Their own wares are much more utilitarian. Exported china is decorated to appeal to the destination buyers.

Teapots made in China often have finely detailed scenes and decorations, or special effects are produced, like in the Celadon set, by impressing rice into the china before firing. When fired, the rice disintegrates, leaving a lovely pattern.

Marking on Chinese teapots is sporadic. They may be marked with Chinese characters, while some have the word "China," and Chinese characters. There are many books listing the standard marks, and many amateurs use them, but it is difficult to decipher

RIGHT ***Lustre scene teapot* has decoration that is quite common with Japanese pieces, yet never loses its appeal. This pot is entirely handpainted. It is marked "Made in Japan". It is 7 in/18 cm high. Other matching pieces were made from the 1930s.**

BELOW ***Gaudy Japanese teapot* is similar in style and character to Geisha Girl items, but it depicts the life of Japanese men. The transfer design was then handpainted for colour and detail. The opposite side shows men travelling; one is on a horse, and others carry supplies or chests on their backs.**

BELOW ***Full-bodied teapot* in transparent china has a demure little spout and a wispy, handpainted flower design. It is unmarked, but was made in China.**

Chinese characters without the help of an expert, and many pieces have marks that are not standard.

Fine china teapots made in any country are sometimes hard to identify if the manufacturer's name is not on the bottom. Once in a while a mark will be under the lid. If you have an unmarked teapot, look for another teapot like it, as it may have a mark.

It has long been said that if you hold a piece of china up to the light and can see the shadow from your hand through it, it is bone china. Bone ash is only one method which produces this translucency in china, but all china will have this characteristic. Fine china teapots will be the more delicate and aesthetically pleasing pieces of your collection.

RIGHT ***Handpainted individual teapot*** **has a moulded handle. The decoration is handpainted over transfers. It was made in Japan. From the base to the top of the handle, this pot is only 4½ in/11 cm high. There are matching, bowl-like cups.**

BELOW ***Side-handled teapot*** **is part of a set that includes four cups without handles. The pieces are decorated with a flying turkey design. Although the set is Japanese, the pot has a lot of Chinese influence. It was bought in Sasebo, Japan, in the early 1970s.**

LEFT ***Japanese house*** **Golden butterflies cover this rectangular pot which resembles a Japanese house. It is unmarked and was made in Japan, but the spout is taken from a Chinese design.**

RIGHT ***Japanese tea jar*** **– a container for tea. The heavy enamel decoration is called "Buff Sharkskin". A tea set was also available. The set was sold in the Butler Brothers catalogue of 1916 and made until the 1920s. The Red Chinese teapot was purchased in China in 1986. The heavy enamel decoration was hand-applied. The colour is called "Emperor Red".**

CHAPTER 4

FLORAL TEAPOTS

"English parties to me mean a deliberate, sustained and very agreeable gaiety, none the worse for the quiet quality of humour. Everyone was afraid of the sudden swoops into sincerity which they had learned to expect of Americans. 'Why do all you Americans, as soon as you have had a cup or two, begin to talk about Life?' asked a friend despairingly."
From England To Me *by Emily Hahn, copyright 1949, Doubleday and Company, Inc.*

Whether it is the genuine affinity of the English with flower gardening, or maybe the association of flowers with a long-awaited spring, floral teapots are plentiful. Nothing evokes images of traditional afternoon tea like that of teapots with floral decoration. Floral teapots fall into three basic categories: transfer printed, factory handpainted, and handpainted.

ABOVE LEFT *Moss Rose set* The teapot, cup, and saucer are not a matching set. They are examples of how the Moss Rose pattern has been made for many years, and used on representative white porcelain (teapot) and fine china (cup and saucer). The teapot, made in the late 1950s, is a musical pot. It is marked on the porcelain with a backstamp, "Made in Japan." The cup was made in China and dates from the 1970s. The saucer dates from the 1960s, and is marked in gold with "Royal Rose, Fine China, Japan". The cup and saucer are made of transparent china. This Moss Rose pattern continues to be a favourite with collectors, and many accessory pieces have been made, along with complete sets of dinnerware. A children's tea set was also made.

ABOVE *Limoges streamlined teapot* was purchased new in Limoges, France, in about 1978. Its modern-looking global shape is not what we might expect a teapot from this traditional French porcelain town to look like.

LEFT ***Moss Rose teapots*** The large pot is a musical teapot playing "Tea for Two". The moss rose design has been produced by many companies in a number of countries, but most common in collections are those from Japan. This teapot has been made since the late 1930s. It is marked with a sticker reading "Wales, Made in Japan", and dates from the late 1950s. The matching set imitates nested tea cosies but the top is a little salt and pepper shaker, and the pot is a jam pot with a notch to fit a spoon. The set is marked "Japan" on a paper label. It is 4¼ in/10.8 cm high.

TRANSFER PRINTED

In this process, a stencil-type method is used to decorate a teapot or other ware with the basic design in one colour. Usually the transfer is done in black or red, but occasionally another colour will be used. Additional colours are brushed into the design, and clay slip may also be applied to give a raised effect.

In England, and to a smaller degree in the U.S., transfer printing was used for the full design, such as in the Blue Willow pattern. The highly collected blue and white wares are mainly transfer printed.

Transfer printing is a term used in the U.S. and England, but with Oriental ware it is called stencilling. A wooden block, or some other hard material, is used to carve or mould the original design. An enamel-type paint is then applied to the block and wiped off, so that the indented areas are filled but the surface is clean. A special paper is then pressed against the block to pick up any enamel left in the design areas. (In the past, a tool like a rolling pin may also have been used. It was passed across the paper applied to the block.) When the paper is removed, it will have picked up just the fine-lined design. The paper is then applied to the surface of the teapot to transfer the design. Sometimes, it is wetted for removal. The piece is then fired to assure bonding of the enamel with the ware. The finished brushwork may be done either before or after

ABOVE ***English sampler*** **teapot looks like a cross-stitched bouquet. This sampler design has been used by many companies, including Royal Doulton, for their Petit Point line, and by American companies, such as E.M. Knowles. It was made in England in the late 1920s, and is marked with a lion. Gold script reads "Old English Sampler".**

ABOVE ***Black-eyed Susan teapot*** **is made in England by Wood & Sons. It bears the common mark of 1970s teapots, and also the pattern name, "Ellgreave". The style, "Centenary, England", is impressed on the bottom. Note the handle, which gives a firm grip, while the spout has just the right curve so as not to drip.**

this last firing, depending upon the type of ware and the paint being used. The gold detail is applied last, because it needs a final firing at a lower temperature.

Transfer printing is still done today with machine-assisted techniques. In some patterns, around the upper lip of a teapot, a slight flaw can be found. This would be a tiny spot where the transfer or object moved slightly during the process, or perhaps where it was smudged.

Today transfer printing is similar to offset printing: the image is taken from the original and transferred to the final product by an interim object. In this process, the design or lettering to be applied does not face backward.

ABOVE ***Miniature Victorian teapot*** **has a matt finish, and is decorated with a transferred basket and flowers, and with handpainted gold accents. It was made in Austria in the 1940s. It is 5 in/12.7 cm high.**

ABOVE ***Sadler roses teapot*** **is highly decorated all over with roses and gold. A matching milk jug and sugar bowl complement this pot; the sugar bowl has no lid, which is common in English sets. The set was made in the 1940s, and is impressed on the bottom with "Sadler, England".**

ABOVE ***Sadler pink oval*** **Dainty roses cover this teapot made by the well-known Sadler company of England. The mark is raised on the bottom; newer pots will have the name "Sadler" stamped on the bottom. This pot is 5½ in/14 cm high, and 10 in/25.4 cm from spout to handle.**

ABOVE ***Georgian roses*** **This lovely oval teapot, decorated with rosebuds, is made by Arthurwood in England. As well as a backstamp, impressed into the porcelain is the shape name, "Georgian". This teapot is 6 in/15 cm high and 10¾ in/27 cm long from spout to handle.**

FACTORY HANDPAINTED

This is a process whereby the design of a teapot or other ware is applied by hand at the factory where it is produced. This could mean all of the design is applied by just one artist, or that it is done in assembly-line fashion with various artists adding different colours and sections.

In the Arts and Crafts Movement, artists employed by various companies designed and decorated their individual ideas. Brush marks – by both well-known and anonymous artists – are often evident on factory handpainted teapots. Take a close look at your floral teapot, and you may notice the brush strokes. If your teapot is marked "handpainted", the work was most likely done in a factory.

ABOVE ***Booth's Floral teapot*** **has a flower in relief as the lid finial, and its transfer design has been handpainted. It is marked on the bottom with "Booths, Silicon China, Made in England, Syevan" – the last word is the pattern name. Other matching pieces were made. The Booth family first began production in 1868, but by 1891 had joined Colclough, and was joined with Ridgway in 1948. The company is now part of Royal Doulton Tableware Ltd. The mark on this pot dates it from 1906 into the 1920s.**

ABOVE ***Wade Flowers teapot*** **has handpainted detail and an applied flower finial. It is marked on the bottom with "Wade, Heath, England," which helps date this pot to between 1938 to 1950. Other matching pieces were made.**

LEFT ***Yellow Noritake*** **is a milk jug, part of a set of dinnerware. The pot is marked on the bottom with a crown, a banner, and a wreath saying "Noritake, handpainted, Japan" and a large "M" inside the wreath. It is 6½ in/16.5 cm high.**

HANDPAINTED

China painting is an age-old art with specific techniques and paints. Since it is applied to a finished blank teapot, a paint is needed that will adhere to the glazed surface and not easily wear off. Most commonly used are powdered paints, which are mixed with oil and turpentine.

A continual study of floral teapots will help you determine whether they have been factory handpainted or painted by an individual. If painted by a china painter, the artist's name may or may not appear on the bottom. It seems that older pots were not always marked, but in the last 20 to 30 years teapots signed by the artist have become more common.

Some collectors specialize in floral teapots; others find these teapots form a collection within their collection. When creating a beautiful table for tea, floral teapots enhance just about any decor. They are as pleasing to the eye as they are perfect for pouring your tea.

RIGHT ***Chocolate pot*** **This large pot looks very much like a teapot, but it is a German chocolate pot (chocolate being a more favoured drink among Germans). It has transfer-painted floral decoration. The pot is 9½ in/24 cm high.**

BELOW ***Rococo-style teapot*** **is ornately decorated with hand-applied and painted flowers and gold. The mark on the bottom shows that it was made in Italy. The interesting thing about this teapot is that the spout has no opening, an obvious factory flaw.**

BELOW ***Wedding cake teapot*** **is hand-decorated, with all the flowers and petals separately applied. This teapot was made in the U.S., possibly by an artist working independently.**

BELOW ***Tall teapot*** **with red flowers and gold trim has magnificent detail. It is unmarked, but was bought in Reims, France, and was made c.1890.**

PORCELAIN TEAPOTS

CHAPTER 5

As explained in Chapter 3, there are two types of porcelain. This chapter deals with the opaque porcelain often called vitreous china. Vitreous means relating to, derived from, or consisting of glass. This is a good description of the durable opaque porcelain used to create many teapots.

One of the most well-known manufacturers of porcelain teapots is the Hall China Company of East Liverpool, Ohio, U.S.A. If you were to break one of their teapots, you would find the porcelain has a hardness similar to glass, while a chip of the glaze has the appearance of broken glass. This hardness is achieved in one high-temperature firing.

Porcelain was first produced in China during the Han dynasty, about 200 years B.C. The Chinese used a white china clay known as kaolin mixed with petuntse – a rock that becomes vitreous when fired at 1,450°C/ 2,725°F. They also used this vitreous rock to form a glaze. The combination of the two only needed to be fired once to achieve a very hard-bodied porcelain with a smooth, glassy surface.

ABOVE LEFT ***Fast rider*** **This teapot was made by the Homer Laughlin China Co. of West Virginia, U.S.A. It is part of their Historical American series made with mulberry-coloured transfers. The designs are scenes painted by the artist Joseph Boggs Beale. Approximately 19 different items were made from the late 1940s to the 1950s.**

ABOVE ***Rooster teapot*** **is handpainted under the glaze and has a locking lid. It holds two cups. It is marked on the bottom "Chowning's Tavern, Williamsburg, Virginia". This teapot is representative of U.S.-made restaurant ware.**

LEFT ***Two Fraunfelter teapots*** **White porcelain shows through the glazed brown ribs of the teapot on the right. It is marked only "Lipton's Tea", yet the same mould was used for the company's line of ware marked with the Fraunfelter name. Both pots date from c.1930. The Lipton's pot was a promotional item commissioned from Fraunfelter. The lids on both pots do not fit well.**

ABOVE ***Pink spattered teapot*** **has very smooth lines with a modern but soft look. It was made by a company called Monterey, in California, U.S.A, in the 1950s. It is 7½ in/19 cm high and 6½ in/16.5 cm across. California pottery and porcelain items have gained popularity in recent years, and continue to be sought after by collectors.**

ABOVE ***Porcelier teapot*** **is made of heavy porcelain and holds about eight cups. The Porcelier Company made many sizes and styles of teapots, including electric pots and pots with aluminium drip-o-lators that fit between the lid and the pot. This pot is marked "Porcelier, Vitreous Hand Decorated China, Made in the U.S.A.". It was made during the late 1930s and into the 1940s.**

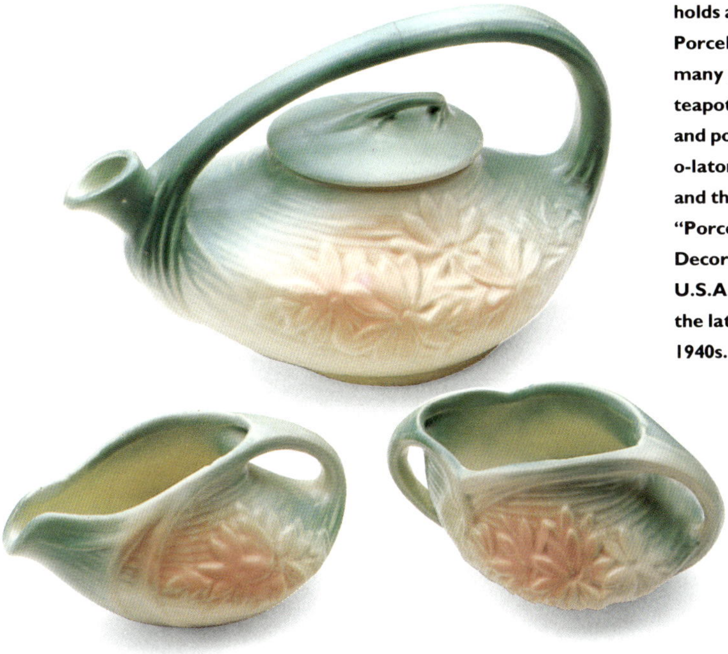

RIGHT ***McCoy daisy teaset*** **in durable white porcelain has a delicate handle. Light colours give the set a Victorian feel. It was made in 1942 and is marked "McCoy".**

There are accounts that Marco Polo first brought porcelain to Europe, though continuing attempts by potters and chemists failed to produce a similar porcelain. In the late 17th century, Augustus II became Elector of Saxony (in modern-day Germany), and one of his first orders to his economic adviser, Von Tschirnhaus, was to find the materials necessary for making fine glass and hard-paste porcelain like that produced by the Chinese.

The chemist J. F. Bottger began working under Tschirnhaus, and by 1708 they had invented a fine white porcelain at Meissen. In around 1720, Bottger combined china stone and clay to produce an even whiter porcelain than the Chinese. While the Meissen factory tried to keep the porcelain ingredients a secret, the turnover of workers from one factory to another made this difficult. By the mid-18th century, other European factories were in competition, producing hard, durable porcelain.

Attempts were made by New World potters to produce this same hard porcelain. It was not until the early 19th century that potteries in America found the right clay and feldspar for porcelain. However, this was also an unstable period for potteries.

The Hall China Company was established in August 1903 by Robert Hall. His son took over the business shortly after its opening, and began experimenting with a process to produce non-lead glazed china in a single-firing process. This was achieved in about 1911, and the company began making institutional ware, including teapots. By 1920 they began a gold decoration, which pushed their teapots to the popularity we know today. The first gold-decorated shapes were the Boston, French, and New York teapots. In 1933 they introduced the famous Autumn Leaf line, offered by the Jewel Tea Company. Autumn Leaf teapots were a premium for purchasing products

BELOW ***Twinspout TeaMaster*** **This cobalt colour is favoured by collectors. The TeaMaster was made by the Hall China Co. in the late 1940s. A pamphlet accompanied this teapot, explaining how to use it. The heading reads "A Vitrified China Combination Tea and Hot Water Pot". It was made for the TeaMaster company, and holds seven cups.**

ABOVE ***Lipton's Tea tin*** **This is a reproduction of the 1915 tea tin used by the Thomas J. Lipton Co. in the U.S. Square-shaped reproductions have been made, and one is currently being sold by mail-order catalogues. The original tin with this lithographed design was made in 1915 and used for a number of years. It was square, much smaller, and held only 225 g/8 oz of tea.**

BELOW ***Lipton teapot*** **was made by the Hall China Co. for Lipton as a premium in the 1930s, and is marked only with an impressed "Lipton's Tea". This pot was produced in many colours. This is Hall China's French shape. Matching milk jugs and sugar bowls were also produced for Lipton, but were taken from Hall's Boston shape.**

ABOVE ***Black Beauty*** **This tall teapot made of a white porcelain has a lot of gold decoration, and is marked in gold on the bottom with "Hand-Decorated, Warranted 22K Gold, Made in U.S.A.". The manufacturer is unknown.**

BELOW ***Franciscan teapot*** **in a smooth-lined style called Tiempo, made from 1949 to 1954. Note the ear-shaped handle, which gives an easy grip when pouring. This California company was bought by The Wedgwood Group in the 1980s. Now their Desert Rose and Apple patterns are made in Japan, although they carry the Franciscan name.**

ABOVE ***Blue Willow*** **This traditional design has been made since the 18th century. This white porcelain teapot was made in the U.S. and holds about six cups. Blue Willow items from various manufacturers blend well together.**

ABOVE ***Music and Tea*** **This teapot plays while it pours, and has obviously poured many a cup because the gold decoration shows much wear. It was made in the U.S. The teapot is 5¾ in/14.5 cm high by 9¼ in/23.5 cm wide.**

such as tea – if you purchased enough tea, you received a free teapot to brew it in.

In the late 1930s, Hall introduced novelty teapots, which today command high secondary market prices. These include the Automobile, the Basket, the Basketball, the Birdcage, the Doughnut, and the Football. Through the years, Hall China has produced over 200 different teapots in approximately 40 different colours. They are still in production, and visitors can take a factory tour, including a visit to their outlet called the Hall Closet (see Useful Addresses).

Since the late 19th century pottery companies throughout the U.S. have produced porcelain teapots. The Knowles, Taylor & Knowles Co., often referred to as KT&K, began in 1853, and by 1872 were producing a white granite ware. The Ohio Valley contains the china-type clay and feldspars needed for porcelain, and many companies were established along the Ohio

River. East Liverpool, Ohio became one of the largest pottery and porcelain production cities. The well-known Homer Laughlin Company had its beginnings in East Liverpool. It soon outgrew two plants, and purchased a third from another company. In 1906, Homer Laughlin headed across the river to Newell, West Virginia, and established another plant, where the company continues today. Its success through the turbulent Depression and post-World War II years can be attributed partly to the company's development of the continuous tunnel kiln in 1923. The kilns previously used were batch-type, or periodic kilns, and were inefficient both in fuel and production time. The Homer Laughlin Company is best known for its line of colourful Fiesta dinnerware, including teapots.

ABOVE ***Downturned spout teapot*** is a dripless teapot made in England by Swinnertons of Staffordshire and carrying the company's mark. It was made c.1950. Also impressed into the bottom of this pot is "Patent Lock Lid" and "No Drip Spout".

ABOVE ***Mickey Mouse & Donald Duck teapot*** is a 1980s creation found at Disney theme parks. The interesting thing about this teapot is that Mickey is pouring a pot of coffee. The backstamp on the bottom reads "Crafted with Pride in U.S.A. by Treasure Craft".

ABOVE ***Wade of England teapot*** In the last ten years, Wade items have grown in popularity as collectibles. This teapot was crafted in the late 1970s. The colourful design is called Orchard, and the pot is marked "Wade, England" on its bottom.

LEFT ***Silver Resist Hexagon*** To make the glaze on this teapot, silver was used, and the pot needs to be gently polished as it dulls from tarnish. The pot was made c.1930. Impressed on the bottom is "Sutherland, Made in England".

LEFT ***Soft Pink teapot*** **The shape of this pot is styled "Rosedawn", although this style comes in other pastel colours, such as blue and grey. It is sized for individual use, although it is 6¼ in/16 cm high. The pot was made by Johnson Brothers in England, and it is marked with the name and a crown.**

RIGHT ***Streamline teapot*** **bears a resemblance to Susie Cooper and Clarice Cliff styles from the Arts and Crafts Movement, which began in the late 19th century. This pot was made c.1930. It is marked "Made in England" and the pattern name: "Streamline, Price Bros." in a wreath.**

ABOVE ***Dub-L-Dekr teapot*** **is just right when serving tea for two, as each person can have an individual pot of tea. A hidden lid is fitted on the lower teapot. Each piece is marked with "Dub-L-Dekr" and "Made in England" raised in the porcelain. A backstamp reads "Heatmaster, Dub-L-Dekr" with patent numbers.**

LEFT ***Johnson Brothers of England*** **produced this scalloped and square teapot, which is part of a dinnerware line with many matching pieces. The footed style gives it a delicate look. "Made in England" is impressed on the bottom of this teapot.**

RIGHT ***Tiffin Tea Liqueur*** **is an unusual liquid for a teapot, but this one is still filled with the original tea liqueur. A label on the back reads: "Tiffin, by a special recipe which combines the finest Darjeeling leaves with pure natural ingredients, the delicate bouquet of this famed tea has been imparted to a delicious liqueur. Known appropriately as 'Tiffin', it has become a favourite for after-dinner sipping or in all sorts of delightful variations. Imported by Shaw Ross Importers, Inc. Miami, Florida, U.S.A., produced and bottled by Anton Riemerschmid, Munich, Germany. Bottle holds 25 fl oz/ 700 ml and is 70% proof".**

European and Japanese potteries have continued to give American factories plenty of competition, although each company tends to have a unique style. While certain Japanese potteries produce a fine artware, they have not perfected the hard porcelain so practical for everyday use. There are many lovely Japanese teapots, but they have an aesthetic more often than a practical appeal.

If you wish to own a teapot you can use every day and do not want to worry about an accidental bump causing damage, look for one made of porcelain. Porcelain is heavier than bone china, but for durability it reigns supreme.

For a list of books on porcelain and, in particular, famous porcelain-producing companies, see Further Reading.

BELOW ***A proper cup of tea*** **Around this teapot's round shape are inscribed directions on how to make a proper cup, including "don't forget the scones". The motif around the upper edge of the teapot is reminiscent of the nursery rhyme "Hey Diddle, Diddle". This teapot was made in 1990 in Japan, and marketed by Boston Warehouse for The New Basics, Workman Publishing.**

LEFT ***Bamboo and butterflies*** **teapot was marketed by Enesco in the late 1970s. It is marked with the pattern name "Butterfly Garden Trellis", and "Made in Japan". Other matching items were also made.**

RIGHT ***The boat shape*** **Many manufacturers have produced this classic lined shape, often called the boat shape. The yellow teapot was made by Bauer, U.S., c.1940; the blue pot is a newer creation made in Japan.**

ABOVE ***Grey and blue teapot*** **is made in Poland, and is marked with a wreath and "P & C". This is a heavy porcelain pot, and it is possibly part of a dinnerware line. The teapot holds six cups.**

Pottery Teapots

Chapter 6

The term "pottery" may be used to describe a factory that produces pottery, porcelain, and china. Many companies produce more than one type of ware, and when researching teapots, you may also find the term "pottery" used generally, referring to everything made by one company. With close attention, you should be able to understand the application of this word without confusion.

Pottery is also the name given to anything made of common clay, sometimes called earthenware. It is the earliest recorded material to be processed into a variety of decorative or utilitarian items. Early pottery was needed as water and food storage jars. Pottery is porous unless a glaze is applied, and it is also opaque, not allowing light to pass through.

To make pottery items there are a few common steps. After the clay and water mixture has been moulded to a desired shape, it must be allowed to dry. This is done either in the sun, naturally in a well-ventilated area, or baked – fired – in a kiln.

ABOVE LEFT ***Greek-style teapot*** **with a hinged lid has a transfer-printed design and is handpainted over the transfer with lustred colours. Its mark is dated from the late 19th to the early 20th century. It stands on a** ***tea tile or trivet*** **– a stand for a hot teapot. This tea tile has had a lot of wear, for it once had gold decoration around the top rim. The manufacturer is unknown.**

ABOVE ***Black German teapot*** **with paper label reads "Bay Keramik, Free of Lead and Dishwasher Resistant" in five languages, including English. The matt glaze and simple shape add up to a pot that is ideal for everyday use. Impressed into the bottom is "W. Germany, Bay". The pot was made in the early 1970s.**

Once dried, a glaze can be applied or the piece can be painted. If glaze is applied, the piece will need to be fired again to turn the glaze into an enamel-type coating. Eastern pottery is often dried naturally and fired only after a glaze has been applied. But Western potters use a process whereby an initial firing is done to dry the clay. The pottery at this stage is usually known as biscuit, from which we derive the term "bisque" to mean ceramic ware left unglazed when finished. The Japanese have produced a lot of bisque pottery, sometimes with a small amount of applied decoration and often with none.

ABOVE *Small Brown Betty* **is the perfect shape for brewing tea. A paper label, still intact, reads "Genuine Old English Brownware Teapot, Ridgway". This is an individual size pot, slightly over 4 in/10 cm high, but the pot has been made in many sizes.**

ABOVE *Wooded scene* **This three-cup teapot was made by the American company Weller, in a majolica style. It is made of a heavy pottery, with crazing in the glaze. It is marked on the bottom and comes either from the company's Glendale or Selma line.**

ABOVE *Frankoma autumn yellow* **teapot on a warming stand. Many other matching Autumn Yellow pieces are available, though Frankoma of Oklahoma discontinued this bright colour in 1990. These pieces are marked with the company name and mould numbers. Note the downward-turned spout for dripless pouring.**

ABOVE *Yellow teapot* **Moulded flowers on this teapot are characteristic of the late 1930s and early 1940s style. On this pot, much crazing tells of a poor match between pottery and glaze. It is marked only with "U.S.A.", but the elongated "S" is common to Nelson McCoy pieces of these years.**

Glazing

A basic description of how pottery is glazed and decorated will help you when collecting teapots.

Glazes are applied in two ways: dipped or sprayed. Glazes are hand-painted by individuals – it is not a factory technique. Dipping is used to coat the inside of a teapot. Spraying on a glaze gives a nice, even coat without blobs or drips.

Under-glaze means that some decoration, and often the pottery's name, was applied before the glaze. You will notice that most marks are limited to a few colours – cobalt, black and red being most common – which withstand the high temperatures of glaze firing.

BELOW ***Leona, Egyptian-style teapot*** **is decorated with coralene enamel. This design makes you think of Cleopatra pouring tea. The teapot is about six-cup size and is marked on the bottom "Leona", while in a banner with a crown over the top is "Gibson & Sons, Ltd., Burslem, England". Under the glaze you can see an impressed mark of "Gibsons".**

LEFT ***Chocolate brown Canadian teapot*** **has tulips and leaves painted over the glaze, and is worn from use. It is a teapot very commonly found on the antiques and collectibles market, especially in the U.S.A. near to Canada. Note that the spout is longer than is commonly found on teapots. This teapot is 6 in/15 cm high and 10½ in/26.7 cm wide.**

RIGHT ***For England and Democracy*** **This unique teapot was made in England and is a favourite among collectors, for it has a lot of marking on the bottom. A rope circles the Union Jack flag and a lion, then reads "World War II, Escorted to U.S.A. by Royal Navy, Made in England". These pots, filled with tea leaves, were made exclusively for exporting as a way to raise money for the war efforts.**

ABOVE ***Canadian two-cup teapot*** **A mottled glaze gives this teapot, made of heavy pottery, interesting detail. Impressed on the bottom is "Tundra, Canada".**

BELOW *Sadler teapot* in a mottled brown, with an upper design that gives a Christmasy feel. The mark on the bottom is a stamp with a crown and banner, which is a later mark than those impressed or raised on the bottom. This teapot is six-cup size and stands 6 in/ 15 cm tall.

LEFT *Black coralene teapot* This brown pottery teapot has a copper-chromed bottom plate so that a trivet or tea tile is not needed, and a hinged lid. It is marked under the handle in an oval: "Alexandra Pottery, Manning Bowman, Made in England".

ABOVE *Salada tea* is an individual teapot that was a premium offered by the Salada Tea Company and made by the Nelson McCoy Pottery Co. c.1930. It is only 5 in/12.7 cm high and 5¼ in/13.3 cm wide. It is marked "Salada Tea, Made in U.S.A.".

RIGHT *The real McCoys* This is a very common shape for McCoy teapots. The pot comes in two different sizes: six cup and two cup, but the design is the same for both, and both are marked "Made in U.S.A." and "McCoy". They were produced from the late 1940s into the 1950s.

Over-glaze is the name given to any decoration applied after the glaze was fired. Most decoration, except for china paints, needs to be fired again, this time at a lower temperature, so it will adhere to the glaze. There is a wider range of over-glaze colours that can withstand this second, low-temperature firing. The Japanese were notorious in their use of an over-glaze enamel paint which easily chipped and peeled to decorate many teapots. But Japanese moriage and coralene designs were fired again. Moriage and coralene are the raised enamel dots or lines applied over the glaze on teapots. While this decoration is sometimes quite worn, this results from everyday use rather than lack of fusion to the glaze.

TYPES OF POTTERY

There are many types of pottery. Stoneware is pottery that is fired at high temperatures. With the best clay, stoneware can be made watertight, making a glaze unnecessary. The stoneware we know today is glazed. Americans love coloured glazes and smooth, shiny surfaces, and wares marketed or made in America reflect this.

Yellow ware is pottery made from yellow-coloured clay. Colours range from buff to an orange-yellow. Yellow ware is normally finished with a clear glaze. Unfortunately, a lot of yellow ware was not marked, making it hard to research. It was primarily made in the United States, Canada and, to a lesser extent, England. Yellow ware was popular from the late 19th century to the early years of this century, possibly because it was inexpensive and made for common household use.

BELOW ***Pear-shaped teapot*** **with a wicker handle was made in Denmark and marked with the country of origin. Teapots made in Denmark are uncommon. Clean lines and a demure spout make this teapot pleasing to the eye. It is made from a brown pottery, and is 8½ in/21.5 cm high to the top of the handle.**

LEFT ***Portuguese teapot*** **has a handpainted design under the glaze, some crazing on the outside, and lots of crazing on the inside. It is marked on the bottom with a backstamp "Made in Portugal". It was made from the late 1950s to the early 1960s.**

RIGHT ***Swirled side-handled teapot*** **has a smooth body. It was made in Japan from fine clay. There is a Japanese mark under the handle.**

ABOVE ***Michigan souvenir wolverines*** **– the Michigan state symbol – appear in relief on this teapot. Indians and deer appear on the reverse side, and there is a transfer design of Mackinac Bridge, which links Michigan's upper and lower peninsulas and opened in 1957. This teapot was made in Japan and is only 5 in/13 cm high.**

Mocha ware is another highly collected form of pottery. This is a category collectors need to study because true mocha ware is not just the pottery decorated with a marbled brown glaze. It was primarily made in England, and sold in America during the first half of the 19th century.

Mocha ware is a heavy pottery, with coffee- and cream-coloured decorations applied by the potter by turning the piece on a lathe using coggle wheels and slip cups. This true mocha ware should not be confused with yellow-ware, graniteware, or ironstone produced in the early part of the 20th century by American potters. A better term for this later ware would be "marbled or mottled ware" or "mottled glaze." Mottled glaze items of pottery have also been produced in Scotland and Wales during the 20th century.

Note: Graniteware is an enamel-covered metal and is not related to pottery. But some graniteware so closely resembles glazed pottery that it needs a second look. I recently saw a teapot in an antique shop I thought was a beautiful glazed pottery item, but upon closer inspection I found it was graniteware.

ABOVE ***Cobalt coralene*** **This style is usually found in a common brown glaze, and this cobalt is a wonderful variation. The teapot is marked "Made in Japan". It was crudely made c.1940s and has pockmarks in the glaze, especially under the lid. It is 6½ in/16.5 cm high and 10 in/25 cm from spout to handle.**

BELOW ***Peacock teapot*** **in a majolica style has a rattan handle over the top, which will stay cool as you pour the tea. It was made c.1960 in Japan. The country of origin is impressed on the bottom.**

RIGHT ***Miniature coralene design*** **on the left is the brown-bodied teapot of a type that was common in the 1940s and 1950s. It is only 3½ in/9 cm high and makes one cup of tea. It is marked on the bottom.**
The majolica-style square teapot on the right has a wonderful scroll design. The body is made of bisque clay and there is crazing overall. It was made c. 1920 and is impressed on the bottom "Made in Japan".

Clay Colours

Pottery teapots are made in many colours, reflecting the naturally occurring types of clay being used by various companies. Colours include off-white, red, reddish brown, light brown, dark brown, yellow, light and dark gray, and black.

The Frankoma Pottery Company of Oklahoma made their wares with a tan-coloured clay called Ada clay, so called because of the area where the clay was excavated. In 1954, they changed to a red brick clay called Sapulpa – the name of the town where the pottery is located and where the red clay is dug.

You will be able to tell what kind of clay soil is found in a certain area by the colour produced by a pottery. Obviously, some areas are not conducive to pottery production. There have been potteries that have attempted to ship clay from other areas, but this is impractical, costly, and often the reason for closure.

Sadler is an English pottery that has produced teapots in both a brown-bodied clay and, in recent years, a white clay. Modern methods may allow for chemicals to be added to a coloured clay, rendering it white. It will not be a true white, but tinted with gray, tan, or buff.

Many Japanese teapots are created with a brown clay, especially those made from the 1930s to the 1950s. Some very fine pottery has come from Japan, but some pieces reveal a poor clay with tiny rocks that leave pockmarks in the glaze.

ABOVE ***Majolica-style teapot*** **On one side is a mouse in relief, but on the reverse is an elephant coloured in cobalt. This pot was made in Japan in the 1940s.**

Colour Glazing and Design

Pottery is naturally a heavy product, but it can withstand boiling water for tea and everyday use. The colours used in glazing pottery teapots are as endless as the colour wheel allows, but some are more desirable to collectors, cobalt blue is probably the favourite. Next in popularity is a true red glaze, and then black. Potteries currently in production watch trends in kitchen colours, and change glazes accordingly.

In 1990, the Frankoma Pottery discontinued their Autumn Yellow colour, which is a golden yellow glaze. Shortly before that, they introduced a Slate Blue colour, which was popular in kitchens of the late 1980s and 1990s. Pfaltzgraff was another company to do the same. Although their Yorktowne pattern just celebrated its 25th year, they have introduced some new lines of stoneware with pastel colours in bolder designs. An example is their Garden Party line, sporting tulips and a green trellis background. Pfaltzgraff is quite collectible, but beware of prices rivalling that of dinnerware no longer in production, such as Fiesta.

Most major department and specialty stores carry pottery or stoneware teapots. Pottery has the heat-retaining qualities perfect for a pot of tea. It is entirely possible that your grandmother's teapot was made from pottery, and maybe even from a local pottery company.

ABOVE ***Chequerboard nested cosy*** **is made in a bisque clay. In cosy sets the milk jug rests upon the teapot to warm the milk, with the sugar bowl on top. This basketweave design is Japanese c.1950.**

Silver, Pewter, and Other Metal Teapots

Chapter 7

Silver Teapots

Teapots made of silver were first produced in England, where the designs were taken from Oriental teapots already in use. One of the earliest examples of a silver teapot is marked with the London date-letter for 1670–71. It was a teapot presented by the East India Company to George Lord Berkeley of Berkeley Castle.

Before fused plate or electroplating was invented, all silver was called "plate". This term came from the Spanish word *plata*, which means silver. Some confusion enters in when the Webster's dictionary listing of the English meaning of plate also includes "1. forged, rolled, or cast metal in sheets of ¼ inch; or 2. a very thin layer of metal deposited on a surface of a base metal".

The process of fusing molten silver to another base metal, especially copper, was accidentally invented in 1742 by Thomas Boulsover. This cutler and button-maker in Sheffield, England, unintentionally spilled silver onto copper, and found they had fused. Many years of experimentation passed before fused plate items were sold on the market.

ABOVE LEFT ***Large oval** teapot* **with a pear wood handle. It was made in London, England, by silversmith Simon Harris in 1798, when the English passion for tea-drinking was well under way. The oval shape remained popular into the 1830s.**

ABOVE ***Bullet teapot* in silver with a wooden handle and finial, and a hinged lid. It was made by London silversmith Edward Pocock in 1729 – under the reign of George II. Bullet-shaped teapots are spherical, tapering to a narrow foot. This one has a straight spout.**

The terms "Old Sheffield Plate" and "Fused Plate" are interchangeable, although not all Sheffield Plate was made in the city of Sheffield. The fused plate method ceased to be used around 1850, and was replaced by electroplating. Beware of silver teapots that bear marks similar to those used on fused plate items, or bearing names such as "Sheffield Plate", "Silver Plate", or "Real Sheffield Plate". These names can be erroneously used to mean Old Sheffield or Fused Plate, thus commanding unreasonably high prices. Take time to research any piece that bears one of the above names.

Sterling silver items continued to be made. Sterling silver is 92.5 parts silver and 7.5 parts copper or other metal, such as nickel or lead. Before the fused plate and electroplating processes were used, silver was used in the church, wealthy homes, and expensive hotels or other establishments. Because of the monetary value, it was for the more affluent. Along with being expensive, sterling silver is a soft metal, and therefore prone to damage in common handling.

But fused plate, dubbed "poor man's silver", was not an immediate success. The wealthy did not want it when they could have solid silver. With society made up predominantly of an upper and a lower class, the latter was more accustomed to pewter or white metal items. As industrialization continued to grow, however, a middle class of citizenry evolved. This middle class helped build a new market range that included fused plate table utensils, such as teapots. Fused plate, and later electroplated silver, were much less expensive and well within reach of the middle class.

Old Sheffield plate was applied in sheets, so if you are trying to identify a piece, run your fingernail gently along a border, or along a bottom rim of a teapot. If the piece is made of fused plate, you should be able to catch the edge of the applied sheet of silver. Old Sheffield plate is not commonly found by collectors. It is more likely you will find what is called Victorian plated ware. Marks bearing the letters "EPNS" or "EPWM" were used on Victorian silver plated items and stand for "Electroplated Nickel Silver" or "Electroplated White Metal".

Silver made in England, whether sterling or plated, has many hallmarks with an involved marking system. There are many good books on English silver marks to help decipher hallmarks. American silver marks are a little easier to identify because most often the

LEFT ***Pear-shaped teapot in silver*** **made in New York by John Brevoort c.1740. It is elegantly decorated, with moulded borders, a domed cover – or lid – with a raised finial, and a graceful octagonal swan-neck spout.**

ABOVE ***The tea kettle*, a larger version of a teapot, can be used to boil water for tea. This Victorian silver tea kettle was made in Birmingham, England, in 1868.**

manufacturers used their name in the mark. If you only find the numbers "925" or something similar, you have solid silver. Some American silver is just marked with the word "sterling". While this should indicate 925 parts silver and 75 parts another metal, this marking cannot be trusted. Another misleading mark is one stating only "silver metal". These two marks could mean any percentage of the metal is silver and another metal. If they appear with a manufacturer's name, it will help verify what kind of silver you have when properly researched. If you are ever in doubt about a silver teapot, have it verified with a silversmith or jeweller.

When attempting to identify silver marks, keep in mind that if the country of origin is included, the item was more than likely made after 1891. If the terms "coin", "premium", "quality", or "standard" are used, the item is American coin silver from the mid-19th century. Although American silversmiths in Baltimore, Maryland, first tried to implement a hallmarking system similar to that of England, the system ground to a halt in 1830. From that time, silversmiths have used their own designs of marking, usually including their name or initials.

While it is not uncommon to find sterling silver teapots and tea sets, the majority found on the antiques and collectibles market will be silver plated. American-made silver-plated teapots are usually marked in some way to indicate that they are plated. The terms "triple plate" and "quadruple plate" often appear. This refers to the number of layers, or thickness, of silver applied to the teapot. Quadruple plate would be four times the standard thickness of silver plating. The more silver electroplated to the pot, the higher the value.

No matter how much silver was plated to a teapot, however, wear is still an issue. It is very costly and often not worth the expense to have a teapot replated. If it is an antique, it may even diminish the value because the pot is no longer in original condition, and original marks may be plated over.

ABOVE ***Silver-plated side handles* The clean lines on these pieces mix a modern and Scandinavian style with side handles. They were made in Italy, and are marked with a horse and the initials "P M". The pot is 9½ in/24 cm high to the finial. The handles are made of wood.**

ABOVE ***Silver-plated teaset*** **Quadruple plate, by Meriden and dated 1934. Hammered beehive all over the body of each piece gives an interesting effect mixed with the traditional shapes and handles.**

Wear of silver plating most often occurs on the handle and lid finial of teapots because of continued use. It is easy to spot the copper colour showing through the silver. Frequent polishing on the body of a teapot will also cause wear. Slight wear is not of great concern, although it diminishes the value somewhat. Beware of teapots with plating that has flaked off, or where 75 per cent of the pot has wear through the plating. Unless there is sentimental value involved, teapots in these conditions should not have high price tags.

The drawback of silver, whether sterling or plated, is that it tarnishes. The bright, reflective shine begins to turn dark and dull. The purer the silver, the better it will retain its shine. Never use the old silver polish, which is abrasive and actually removes a minute amount of the silver, to restore the shine. Products are available to keep your silver sparkling without polish damage. A jeweller or silversmith, or staff in the silver department of a large store, will recommend a brand.

Never use any harsh cleaner or abrasive scrubbing pad on your silver or silver-plated teapots. Try warm soapy water and a sponge to remove fingerprints or dust. Always use a soft cloth when applying a cleaner or polishing up, to prevent surface damage. Protective coatings can be applied to silver to preserve it from tarnishing, but this is only recommended if you do not plan to sell your teapot or tea set. Be sure to read the product directions before attempting to preserve your silver. Check with a local silversmith or a jeweller first; you may want to have this process done by a professional.

Pieces in a tea set from the early 19th century often do not match. This has happened for one of two reasons. The first is that tea was not always taken with milk or sugar, so milk jugs and sugar bowls were not needed. Pieces were added as customs and preferences changed. The second is that lower to middle class people often could not afford a whole tea set. A period of many years sometimes passed between a teapot being made and someone commissioning the silversmith to make the matching pieces. Various pieces of a tea set might even be procured from different silversmiths, especially in America, where people were on the move.

Tea sets from the late 19th century into the early 20th century more often matched, and included any number of items: teapot, milk or cream jug, sugar bowl, coffeepot, tray, tea caddy, warming stand, teaspoons, tea strainer, and mote spoon (used for skimming the tea). The more detailed the decoration or chasing on a teapot or tea set, the more valuable it is. Over the years, pieces of a tea set often became separated. Collectors especially desire sets that include a milk jug, a sugar bowl, and a tray; other items are a bonus.

Collectors will also find that silver and silver-plated teapots and tea sets are most common in the U.K. and in the eastern states of the U.S.A., although they are found almost everywhere. Silver tea sets are still offered for sale in more exclusive stores. When serving tea for more than one, tradition calls for tea brought on a silver tray bearing a silver (or silver-plated) tea service.

Pewter Teapots

The outer finish of pewter teapots may range from a dull gray to a shine similar to silver. Pewter is made with varying combinations of tin, lead, copper, and other metals. The more lead used to make the pewter, the darker or duller the finish. Pewter teapots with a satin finish have greater amounts of tin.

Pewter teapots have impressed marks like silver marks. Silversmiths and metalworkers often worked with more than one type of metal. When researching the mark on a piece of pewter, try looking in a book on silver marks. Unfortunately for collectors, much pewter is not marked.

Pewter has been made for centuries, but the era of greatest production in pewter teapots and coffeepots was from 1825 to 1850. Pewter pots were made before and after this time, but by 1850 silver-plated items surpassed pewter in affordability.

A great deal of the pewter found today is really Brittania metal. Brittania contains no lead, but is composed of tin, antimony, and copper in varying proportions. Brittania could also be shaped by spinning it on a lathe around a wooden chuck, something not easily done with common pewter. Also, Brittania could be electroplated with silver.

ABOVE ***Darkened pewter* pot has a hinged lid which opens. It is marked with Roman numerals xxxvii. There is a strainer inside, so while this pot looks more like a coffeepot, it was intended for tea. It is almost 8 in/20 cm high and marked "New Amsterdam Silver Co., Pewter".**

LEFT ***Bail handled pewter pot* The bail is wrapped in copper on this pot. It was made in Japan and was marked "M.H". in a diamond. It holds 1 cup and is 3½ in/9 cm high.**

Some other advantages of Brittania ware are that it was tougher and longer-wearing. Pewter is naturally soft, and prone to dents or even sagging with weight. Brittania metal did not need to be as thick as pewter. This made for lightweight teapots. Brittania can also be polished to a wonderful shine almost indistinguishable from silver. Brittania ware with a dark colour may have been made with an alloy intended for silver plating. No amount of polishing will bring a shine.

The handles and spouts of pewter and Britannia teapots were soldered; other parts were also sometimes soldered, such as a flanged base, an upper rim, or feet. The lid was moulded separately, and the finial added. The metal conducted heat rapidly, therefore handles and finials were often made of wood to prevent burning. Because of the strength of Brittania metal, more examples have survived from the 19th century. When researching, check sources dealing with silver or pewter because most have a section on Brittania metal. Pewter teapots were produced in the 20th century, but nickel silver or silver plating rapidly took over the market.

To clean pewter or Brittania ware, use non-abrasive cleaners. Bear in mind that many metal polishes are abrasive. Ask a silversmith or the staff in the silverware department of a store to recommend a product that will safely clean and remove some of the dullness from pewter. A non-abrasive spray bathroom cleaner will also work. Use a scrubbing pad made for Teflon-coated pans or glassware.

Other Metal Teapots

While silver or silver-plated teapots and tea sets evoke images of traditional afternoon tea, teapots have been fashioned from many other metals. They can be found made from copper, aluminium, brass, tin, and cast iron. Because of the ability of copper to withstand repeated heating and cooling, copper teapots are common. Copper has also long been used in combination with other alloys, such as tin and brass. Copper-clad bottoms of kettles are designed to conduct heat quickly and evenly. The process for smelting aluminium was not refined until the early 20th century and the majority of aluminium teapots found today date from the 1950s, although they were made as early as the 1930s. Aluminium, made from the compound element bauxite, is very light and conducts heat, yet it is tough and durable. It is very suitable for teapots, although handles are often fashioned from another material, such as Bakelite, wood, or plastic.

Brass teapots are commonly produced in India, although plenty have been produced in other countries. Brass has been used since ancient times, and is an alloy of copper, zinc, and other metals. Both brass and copper tarnish with time, and need periodic polishing. Marks of manufacture can be found on brass teapots, but are not easy to research. Teapots made in India commonly bear the country's name. Indian craftspeople take pride in hand engraving their brass teapots and other items, and the tooled engraving is easy to recognize.

During the Victorian era, large brass teapots on warming stands were popular. The 1901 catalogue of Harrod's department store in London offered many styles and sizes of such teapots. Three styles were offered with floor stands that held the teapot at armchair height. Others have pivoting stands that assist with pouring. Harrod's teapots were offered in plain, hammered, or repoussé finishes (that is, shaped or hammered from the opposite side to create a design in relief.)

BELOW ***Brass teaset*** **is made in India. All pieces are hand-etched. It is marked with paper labels on each piece. The teapot is 10 in/25 cm high, with a Bakelite handle.**

ABOVE ***Individual aluminium pot*** **made by Swan Brand in England. This teapot is commonly found in specialty or British import shops in various sizes. Its handle and finial are in Bakelite. The teapot holds approximately two cups, and is marked "The Carlton".**

Teapots made of brass or copper have been made in recent times, so beware of those being passed off as antiques. A copper teapot marked "Japan" or "Taiwan" is not an antique. A gooseneck-styled copper teapot with a wooden bail handle was filled with a floral arrangement by Florists' Transworld Delivery in the early 1980s; these make fine additions to your collection, but do not pay the prices you would pay for antiques.

Cast-iron and tin teapots are not as common as those made in other metals, but many examples can be found. The highly collected "Japanned Ware" is a tin tole-painted ware. In America, the Pennsylvania Dutch Community made painted tole items, including many teapots that are highly collectible today. The height of popularity for cast iron was in the second half of the 19th century. Cast-iron kettles were a household necessity, and sat upon the wood stove or steam radiator to keep hot water handy. This also served as a natural humidifier. Cast-iron kettles are still manufactured today. Cast-iron teapots are not as common, but can be found. More often than not the inside was given a protective, heavy enamel coating. Cast iron is naturally porous, providing the perfect place for mineral build-up and corrosion.

Metal teapots have been produced in abundance in the last two centuries, and each type has its advantages and drawbacks for making tea. If you plan to add a copper or brass teapot to your collection for aesthetic reasons, there is no need to consider how well it will brew tea. Various types of metal impart a metallic flavour to tea. The favourites among tea drinkers are silver and silver plate teapots as they are least likely to affect tea flavour.

The advantages of metal teapots are their durability and strength in everyday use. With many alloys and metal compositions to choose from, collectors should be able to add variety to other teapot categories.

LEFT ***Brass teapot*** **with a movable bail handle is decorated with a hand-hammered design. It holds one cup and is 3 in/7.6 cm high.**

RIGHT ***Small India teapot*** **with matching cup that doubles as a stand. The hinged lid opens for making only a small amount of tea. A paper label inside the cup reads: "Made by Craftsmen whose art has been handed down through the generations; India Brassware, nickel plated, black enamelled, and hand engraved".**

ABOVE ***Gunshell*** **This brass pot is made from recycled gunshells and marked on the bottom with a winged Phoenix and foreign letters; possibly this was the mark originally on the large shell used for the base. The pot holds about one cup.**

LEFT ***Russian samovar*** **is a reproduction made in 1980. An old Russian samovar, privately procured and sold, was used to have this version reproduced in Turkey, and the copy is marked the same as the original. It is made of brass-lined tin, and a warmer on the bottom keeps the large pot of water hot. A tube runs up through the middle and exhausts through the top teapot holder, helping to keep the small teapot warm. The Russian tea tradition is to make a very strong tea in the smaller pot, pour a conservative amount into a cup, and then add hot water to make the desired strength.**

ABOVE ***Spigot teapot*** **is made from a chromed copper, and is an electric teapot. A teaball rests inside, and can be pulled up out of the tea by a ball and chain at the top of teapot. Patent numbers on the bottom of the base date from 1903 to 1910, and the pot is marked "General Electric Company". Handles, spigot handle, and ball feet are made from wood. The teapot holds from four to six cups.**

RIGHT ***Black teapot and stand.*** **This teapot is made of cast iron, but is enamel-coated inside. It is shaped like a Japanese house, and ivy leaves decorate one side. A warming candle fits into the bottom. The pot has a removable strainer of aluminium.**

TINY TEAPOTS

CHAPTER 8

INDIVIDUAL-SIZED TEAPOTS

This size of teapot normally holds one cup, sometimes slightly less, and may brew as much as two cups. The size is perfect for making tea just for one. Not all teapots of this size were intentionally made for brewing tea. Individual pots were made as souvenirs, novelties, commemoratives, or gifts. Teapots of this smaller size are wonderful to collect because they take up much less room than their six-cup counterparts.

Individual-sized teapots are often referred to as "mini-" or "miniature" teapots, but those terms should really be used for teapots too small for serving tea in any capacity. One- to two-cup teapots have been made in a wide variety of designs and mediums in every country producing teapots at all. This is definitely an area that lends itself to a collection within a collection.

The first individual-sized teapots were Chinese Yixing teapots (see Chapter 2, Figural Teapots). Given the fact that tea was, for a long time, an expensive and special commodity, only small amounts were brewed at any given time. One strong little pot of tea might produce three or four cups when only a small amount is poured into a cup and then diluted with hot water. This changed in the late 18th and early 19th centuries, causing teapots to grow in size.

While the custom in Victorian England was to serve afternoon tea to a small group, which meant using a large teapot, tea merchants still shipped small teapots with their tea to encourage tea drinking. Thus the individual-sized pot has been made for generations.

A small teapot, rather than a complete tea service, was transported more easily to the New World as the American continent grew. American potters and metalworkers have not neglected this size of teapot, which fits easily on a tray, a small table or a desk.

ABOVE LEFT *Motto ware teapot* is made of Torquay, a unique type of red clay pottery made in the late 19th century and up until the 1960s in Devon. This teapot is marked with "Watocombe", which is the pottery name. This ware is famous for the mottos that were inscribed on each piece. The motto on the opposite side of this teapot says "Tea seldom spoils when water boils".

In this book, some one- and two-cup teapots have been included in most chapters. They are referenced in the same manner as larger teapots: first look for information about the mark or backstamp.

Children's Teapots

Going to Tea
You're going out to tea today,
Be careful what you do;
Let all accounts that I hear
Be pleasant ones of you.

Don't spill your tea or gnaw your bread,
And don't tease one another.
And Fanny mustn't talk too much
Or quarrel with her brother.

Now mind your manners, children five,
Attend to what I say;
And then perhaps I'll let you go
Again another day.

These words of wisdom for a children's tea are from Kate Greenaway (1846–1901), a popular Victorian author and artist.

FROM LEFT TO RIGHT ***Flat brown teapot*** is a modern Yixing teapot that developed a rich patina. It was given to a collector by a Chinese friend, who considered this teapot her most prized possession. ***Floral teapot with wicker handle*** is only 3½ in/9 cm high, not including the handle. ***Silver chased teapot*** is an ornate Yixing-style pot dating from the late 1970s and early 1980s.

ABOVE ***Baby blue Wedgwood*** is a similar colour to the company's blue jasperware, but this set has a high-gloss glaze. All pieces are impressed with "Wedgwood" on the bottom. This is a children's set made in 1943, and intended for use in a nursery. The milk jug is larger than the teapot, an arrangement typical of English sets: more milk was needed when serving children, and less tea. It is likely that there were other pieces to go with this set, including teacups, saucers, and plates.

ABOVE ***Miniature redware*** teapot is decorated with coralene flowers and striped detail. There is no marking on this teapot, but it is either from China or Japan. Designed for individual use, the pot mimicks the Yixing teapots that were made in China for many centuries.

BELOW ***Charles and Diana*** This commemorative teapot is marked 1981, the year of the marriage of the English royal couple. It is made of brown pottery and decorated with striping and clear glaze. Impressed on the bottom is "Wales" and an "M" inside a "C". The teapot is only 3 in/7.5 cm high.

ABOVE ***Floral children's set*** is decorated with transferred flowers and handpainted details. Both teapot and milk jug are marked with the country of origin – Germany.

LEFT ***Skating monkey* is part of a children's dinnerware line produced by Edwin M. Knowles China Co. The teapot was made in the U.S., and is marked on the bottom with a basket or pot that says "semi-vitreous".**

RIGHT ***Dotted round pot* is made for individual use. It was made in Japan of a fine translucent china. This pot is only 3½ in/9 cm high.**

During the Victorian era, roughly the second half of the last century, well-to-do families would furnish a nursery with things of just the right size for the children. While the adults were served tea formally in the parlour or meals in the dining-room, children were served in their nursery. This included high tea, which often took the place of dinner and was really an early supper. This practice necessitated child-sized china and dishes, including tea sets.

Teacups were made the right size for children of three years and older. The teapot, sugar bowl, and milk jug were all of similar proportions. Children's tea sets commonly found today were made after the turn of the century, and may include extra serving pieces, adding to their collectibility.

In the 20th century, the tradition of providing a nursery and china just for the children has slowly faded away, yet tea sets are a favourite in pretend play. Children's tea sets are easily distinguished from other toy, doll, and miniature sets because of their size. If the teapot will pour two or more small servings and the cups will hold three to four fluid ounces or about 110 millilitres, you can be sure you have a children's set. Any smaller than this, and the set would be considered toy or doll size.

At first glance, some children's tea sets look like demitasse (French coffee cup) size – only slightly smaller than those used for adults. The size of the teapot, sugar bowl, and milk jug will help determine that the set is really meant for children.

Many teapots and tea sets for children have been fashioned after adult sets of the same pattern. This was done in the late 19th century but more so in the 20th century. This practice carried over from porcelain and china tea sets to glass, plastic, and tin. These tea sets were intended for play or childhood tea parties; children could mimick adults, and at the same time enjoy the gaiety of tea time.

Teapots and tea sets for children made since the turn of the century can easily be found from German, English, and American potteries, but those from other European countries are not as common. Japan has kept up a running competition and still exports children's tea sets today.

In the late 1980s, the trend was revived for children's teas and tea parties. Major toy companies such as Fisher-Price produced tea sets from heavy, durable plastic. Two different sets – one for very young children, the other for five years and older – have been made in which the cups change colours to look like they contain tea, and jam magically appears on the tea cakes. Barbie tea sets have recently been made in china and plastic.

Since about the 1930s, many tea sets have been produced depicting cartoon characters, popular dolls, and Disney themes. The majority of these have been made in Japan, some of high-quality china and others more crudely.

There are many collectors who specialize in children's things and especially tea sets. Some excellent reference books are available (see Further Reading). Collecting the playthings of children conjures memories and feelings of youth. A majority start with an interest in the tea set from their own youth, and find similar sets appealing. If you collect children's tea sets, take the time to use a favourite with a youngster.

TOY AND DOLL TEAPOTS AND TEA SETS

Toy and doll tea sets can be described as those small enough for a doll to use (if a doll indeed could), or for a child to pretend with dolls and stuffed animals. While most can hold liquid, they are not big enough to brew tea. Their charm is in their exquisite size rather than their usefulness.

While teapots and other items intended for children's use were predominantly made in sets, this starts to change with toy and doll items. Children's sets often included many extra pieces, but with toy and doll tea items it may just be a small teapot. The common toy set is just a teapot with two cups and saucers. Other sets include a teapot, milk jug, and sugar bowl; where the make-believe tea was to be poured is not clear. An example is an English gold lustre tea set that includes a teapot, milk jug, and sugar bowl on a tray with just one lonely cup and saucer. Because of their small size, these teapots or sets were prone to damage and loss. The button-sized lid to many a toy teapot has been lost in use.

Since toy and doll tea sets were children's things, this is the best place to start when researching such items. Sources listing doll accessories is another place where small teapots and tea sets would be listed. They were items meant for play, and therefore complete sets and those with little or no wear are hard to find. Collectors must settle for wear on gold decoration or cracks and chips in some pieces. Evidence of much use on a toy teapot or tea set brings a pleasant link with the past and present. Little fingers spent wonderful hours pretending to have tea – most likely with a beloved doll or teddy bear.

LEFT *Boxed tea set* Wear on these handpainted pieces of bisque porcelain tells us that many children enjoyed the use of this tea set. It was made from the late 1890s to the early 1900s. Note the detailed printing on the box.

ABOVE *Dolly Dingle tea set* comes in a box marked "1983" and is made in Japan. All pieces are marked and have poses of Dolly Dingle. This set is made for real tea parties.

RIGHT *Tea for five* set shows a lot of wear on the gold and floral decoration. The cups are shaped like mugs, though this set probably dates from the early 1900s. The pieces are not marked, but may have been made in Germany.

Miniature Teapots

There is a certain enchantment with anything in miniature proportions, and even people who do not collect tiny things are intrigued when confronted with the minuscule size. The charm of miniature teapots is in imagining drinking tea on such a ridiculous scale.

Miniature items are not intended for use or for play. Many are so small they are hard to handle without feeling you will drop the minute thing. One of the smallest teapots is made of blown glass ¼ in/6 mm high; others range from 1–1½ in/2.5–3.8 cm high. The detail on these mini teapots can be astounding.

Miniature teapots are best displayed and stored in wall-hung curio cabinets, or on a shelf, secured with wax especially made for collectibles. Look for it at your local craft or hardware store. It will not damage items, is removable, and will safely fix tiny things to a shelf.

Miniature teapots and tea sets are novelty items, and originally were inexpensive. Some mimick actual large teapots, such as the Cadogan teapot or Blue Willow pattern. Others are simply intended to be gift items. Mini teapots can be found from many different countries, but they have been made mainly in Japan. Because of their tiny size, many are not marked and are hard to research.

Miniature teapots have and continue to be made in every conceivable medium, including brass, wood, glass, and china. One tiny teapot is fashioned from rolled paper, an art form called scrolling. This teapot is only ½ in/13 mm high, and has a matching cup and saucer. Blown-glass teapots are an easy design for glass artists, and can be found at country fairs or craft shows. New miniature teapots or tea sets can be found wherever crafts are sold, and in catalogues offering doll's house supplies.

Miniature teapots are so small they can be easily overlooked when searching at antiques shops, flea markets, or bring and buy sales. Take the time to look closely in glass cabinets and curio trays, because this is where most will be kept. Try asking dealers if they have any tiny teapots, because these little items are often hiding under or behind a larger collectible.

When the space on your shelves is already filled with beautiful teapots, there will still be room enough for miniatures. And you can be sure that anyone observing your collection will be amazed at the tiniest of teapots.

Souvenir Teapots

Souvenir teapots evoke memories of places near and far, while encouraging the tea time tradition. Many tourist stops still offer a variety of souvenir teapots. Antiques shops and small-town general stores are also fine places to locate souvenir items.

An enormous number of souvenir teapots has been and continues to be made in Japan. The ones made from about 1930 to 1950 are easy to distinguish from those made in the last 30 years. The scenes on older ones were transfer printed, then handpainted, and have a lot of gold decoration. Newer scenes or pictures depicting a certain place are done with a thicker enamel and modern artwork. The trim may be in gold but often takes one of the colours used in the design, such as black or red.

The collecting of souvenir items has grown since the 1980s. While collectors may want to specialize in souvenirs from just one country or area, examples are available from other places. Some depict the country of origin, while others are intended to commemorate a visit to a famous spot.

If you are looking for older souvenir teapots, they will be found in the same places as other pots: antiques shops, flea markets, local fund-raising sales, and second-hand shops. Most are marked, but a few will be harder to research. An example of an unusual marking is a teapot only decorated with a rooster, but with a mark on the bottom reading: "Chowning's Tavern, Williamsburg, Virginia". The reference is to the tavern, but it is doubtful that this teapot was made in Williamsburg. Upon examination, the porcelain body and glaze is much like restaurant ware made in the U.S., but where the teapot was produced is unknown.

Souvenir teapots do not command the higher prices of fine china teapots, and therefore are a good specialty field. A souvenir collector's network has been established called *Antique Souvenir Collectors News*.

ABOVE ***Precious Moments* A** tea set on a stand. It includes a teapot, a cup, and a saucer. The set is dated 1989 and marked "Precious Moments, Samuel J. Butcher". It is licensed and marketed by Enesco Imports Corp. The teapot is 2 in/5 cm high; the total height of the set on the stand is 6 in/15 cm.

ABOVE ***Dainty floral tea set*** sits on a tray. This set is made of a fine china. A paper label on the bottom of the tray says "Made in Japan". This set was made in the late 1950s.

BELOW ***Gold tea set*** is just the right size for this handmade, antique replica doll, which belonged to the author's grandmother. The tea set was made in England around the turn of the century.

ABOVE ***Japanese wicker-handled teapot*** This pot is 3¼ in/8 cm to the top of the bail handle, and has floral decoration handpainted over glaze. The pot is not marked, but it was made in Japan in the late 1930s to the early 1940s.

ABOVE ***Miniature Chinese teapot*** was purchased in Okinawa in 1986. The removable lid is no bigger than a tiny button. The teapot is unmarked. It is only 1¼ in/3 cm high, including the handle. The pot has a stand only 1½ in/3.8 cm high.

ABOVE ***Occupied Japan* A** teapot from a child's teaset in the famous Blue Willow pattern. Stamped on the bottom is "Made in Occupied Japan". The set includes cups, saucers and plates. It was made from the late 1940s to the early 1950s.

ABOVE ***Half-circle copper teapot.*** Although this pot is hollow and has a hole in the spout, the lid – with a glass bead for a finial – is fixed and does not open. It was made c.1930 and marked "China". It is just 1½ in/3.8 cm high.

GLASS TEAPOTS

"Glass is more gentle, graceful, and noble than any metal and its use is more delightful, polite, and sightly than any other material at this day known to the world."
By Antonio Neri, 1612, from A Short History of Glass, *Chloe Zerwick, The Corning Museum of Glass, 1980.*

Evoking the pleasure of tea, the above reference seems directed toward glass teapots. An overlooked medium for the tea vessel, glass teapots give a transparent value that no other teapot can claim. In what other sort of teapot could one watch the tea brew and stop the process at just the desired strength?

Glass history has been traced back to the days of Moses leading the Israelites out of Egypt. Yet glass teapots are basically a 20th-century invention. The examples made before this century were delicate pieces of art, not able to withstand the boiling hot water required for brewing tea.

At the turn of the century, most chemical and laboratory glass came from Germany. Although German manufacturers were trying to improve their glass, the Corning Glass Works of Corning, New York, were working toward the same goal. The lantern globes they produced were prone to frequent breakage from extreme weather temperatures. With perseverence, Corning invented a heat-resistant glass globe.

About this same time, Corning hired Dr. J. T. Littleton. With help from his inquisitive and persistent wife, the idea of glass bakeware was conceived. His wife first experimented with their glass by baking cakes in cut-down battery jars. When she showed her husband that it worked, the lab began research to develop glass cookware. Within two years the cookware was ready for marketing.

A teapot was designed, but not offered for sale immediately. In 1915, the first item to be marketed was a pie plate; it was called Pyrex, from "pie-right" ("just right for pies"). The first Pyrex items had a faint brown

LEFT ***Pyrex stove top teapot*** **will keep tea warm after brewing. It was made in the early 1950s as part of the Pyrex Flameware line, and bears a flame mark. It is marked on the bottom with "6 cup, Pyrex, Made in U.S.A.". Note the glass handle.**

ABOVE ***Individual teabagger*** **is made by Pyrex for Teakoe Teamakers. Once the tea has brewed, the bag is pulled up through the slot and strings wrap around the button on the handle, keeping your tea from becoming strong or bitter. A metal frame keeps the heat of the pot off the table. It is marked with "2 cup. Made in U.S.A.".**

colour, and it was not until 1936 that a new formula was developed to create clear glass. Teapots were introduced in 1923, and by 1925 there were four different shapes and sizes. A Pyrex tea tile was also produced. By the late 1930s, an etched design was added to Pyrex glassware, including teapots.

Glass teapots are not as rare as you might think, but they are harder to find in perfect or mint condition. They were meant for regular use, and therefore proved susceptible to accidental chips or cracks.

The Corning Glass Company has produced many types of teapot throughout the years, but other companies made them, too. Sears offered a line called Flamex Glass Cookware, which included a whistling teakettle. Another line, called Maid of Honor, offered a teakettle and a teapot with a lock-on lid. The Glassbake and Fry companies also produced glass teapots. A German teapot – the Jena – is currently being sold with its own glass warming stand and tea infuser. The advantage of a glass teapot is that it can withstand stovetop heat to keep the pot warm.

ABOVE ***Simply Clear teapot*** **was made in the late 1970s. It has a sticker stating "Made in Korea". It stands 7 in/18 cm high.**

ABOVE ***Pyrex teapot*** **An example from the famous glassmaker, this smooth-lined, undecorated glass teapot is a style first made in 1929 and produced into the early 1940s. Marked on the bottom and around the lid with "Pyrex."**

CHRISTMAS TEAPOTS

With no other holiday do we invest so much time, effort, and money as Christmas, so is it any wonder that teapots in yuletide motifs continue to grow in popularity? Teapots depict other major holidays such as Easter, Thanksgiving, and the Fourth of July.

Holiday gatherings and teas are so closely related that in 1982 Tom Hegg wrote a rhyming story, *A Cup of Christmas Tea*. Set to the traditional cadence of "T'was the Night Before Christmas", this is a sweet tale about visiting an elderly aunt for a cup of tea. The cover, illustrated by Warren Hanson, depicts a teacup and saucer in a holly and berries design in watercolour, while inside is the matching teapot. In 1990, the teacup and saucer were marketed by Waldman House and made in Taiwan. In 1992 came the matching teapot, and the following year a matching greeting card was printed with the last line of the book, "And then we settled back and had a cup of Christmas tea."

One of the earliest Christmas teapots recorded is that of Father Christmas made by Sadler of England in the late 1930s. No doubt others were made before this time, but this narrow theme never became popular. During the Victorian era who would purchase a teapot only to be used for a short season of the year?

LEFT ***Soldier for tea*** **has lots of handpainted detail. It was made in China in 1992 and marketed by the Russ Berrie Company.**

ABOVE ***Fros-Tea teapot*** **has coloured detail handpainted over the glaze in strong enamel. This pot does not pour well because of the shape of the spout. A paper label on the bottom says "Holidays, Himark, made in Taiwan". This teapot has been marketed in many mail-order catalogues.**

RIGHT ***Christmas bear*** **is a large teapot made in Korea and marketed by Fitz & Floyd. This company has marketed many Christmas teapots, and in recent years has offered three or four new pots each year. This pot is dated 1991 and a mark states that it holds 28 fl oz/795.5 ml. Matching cups became available in 1993.**

Holiday-themed teapots have gained in popularity since the 1950s, and each year brings novel themes to choose from. Fitz and Floyd have especially contributed to the Christmas-styled teapots; their pots include a Christmas teddy bear and a Dickens-inspired Victorian house teapot with matching creamer and sugar bowl.

Many teapots of the past, while not deemed as holiday items, had Christmas-like designs, especially in red and green. An example might be decoration of green leaves and red berries, although the leaves would not be in the traditional holly shape.

While a simple red teapot fits Christmas decor, others are elaborate renditions, only taking the outward appearance of a teapot. For instance, the Holiday Hideaway teapot marketed by House of Lloyd is a mouse house cutaway of a teapot; battery operation lights the moving figures to a soft music box sound.

Practically any character or traditional item of Christmas has been moulded into a teapot. New in 1993 were a teapot and matching cups shaped like a glossy Christmas tree bulb, available in metallic finishes of red, green, or gold. Many versions of a Christmas tree teapot have been made, some with matching creamer and sugar bowls.

Other holiday-theme teapots that have been collected include a heart pierced with an arrow, Easter bunnies in many styles and sizes, and even a turkey teapot.

Holiday-themed teapots are not as common as some other categories, but you should be able to collect a different one for each season.

RIGHT ***Rudolph the Red-Nosed Reindeer*** **is shown in two different versions, both made in Japan and having fawns as handles and sleigh bells as lid finials. Handpainted detail over the glaze on both sets tends to chip and wear off. The black set is a nested cosy – the milk jug is missing. Neither piece is marked.**

ABOVE ***Elf teapot*** **A paper label, still attached, reads "Golden Crown, E & R, Western Germany", "E & R" stands for Ebeling & Reuss Co. out of Pennsylvania – an import company. This label dates this teapot from the mid-1950s.**

ABOVE ***Holiday hideaway*** **is a musical teapot. Momma and Poppa mice are dressed in Santa outfits, and all four characters move when the music plays. The musical box winds up, but battery operation is required for the light and movements. The pot was made in China in 1992.**

ABOVE RIGHT ***Aluminium teapot*** **is enamel-covered, made in the late 1970s, and marked "Made in Taiwan". The simple pear shape of this teapot is pleasing to the eye. The body is covered with enamel, the lid is wood, and the handle has been wrapped with vinyl for a cool touch.**

Collecting Guidelines

Chapter 9

Setting the tradition of tea-drinking aside, teapots have a charm all their own. No other china, pottery, or porcelain object combines function and form in quite the same way. While some teapots have strayed as far as possible from function, most bear three unique components.

The first is the handle, a characteristic of the teapot that has been shaped and moulded over time. When handling a teapot, one senses a sure hold on the pot, much like the grip one would hope to have on life. Humans seem to have an innate desire for control, and for the feeling that we have things within our grasp. Teapots allude to this feeling by providing an easy grip.

Secondly, the eye-pleasing body of a teapot has been known to lure even those who do not normally collect teapots. The artistry of potters from early China to the present day has led to the development of teapots with bulbous bodies not just to brew the perfect pot but to enhance the total experience of tea-drinking. Have you ever tried to pick up a teapot without being tempted to touch its body?

And third, teapots are most unique in their spout. While coffeepots are furnished with spouts, their spouts tend to be longer and start closer to the base of the pot. More often, coffee comes straight from the coffee maker or carafe. Tea is traditionally poured from the pot more often than coffee, thus the need for a practical spout. The teapot spout rises from the body of the pot, giving the tea leaves or tea bags a place to settle but not clog the inside opening.

The spout of a teapot gently symbolizes the tradition of tea as a social occasion. The intimate conversation and relaxing atmosphere, the give and take of conversing and listening, are often just as refreshing as the tea and biscuits. It is impossible to gaze upon a teapot without imagining the pouring of tea.

ABOVE LEFT ***The back* of a German tea/chocolate pot – some pots have a definite front and back.**

TEAPOT HANDLES

ABOVE **Good handles for gripping a teapot: a dripless brown teapot, England.**

ABOVE **A handle from a pot made in Italy.**

ABOVE **An ear-shaped handle from Franciscan Tiempo.**

STARTING A COLLECTION

The majority of collectors begin the same way I did – someone gave me a teapot. In my case it was a teapot that had belonged to a great aunt. After placing it on the mantelpiece I thought, "Teapots are charming, I think I'll collect a few more". The "few" continued to grow, and now there are more than 400 in the collection, including many miniatures.

A collection does not have to be large to bring enjoyment. One of the most common mistakes of new collectors is to buy every teapot they see. There is nothing wrong with this approach, except that in time you will find you have bought teapots that do not thrill you any more, and you will have to "weed out" your collection. More consideration from the start will help you build an enjoyable collection.

The most cherished teapots are often those received from family or friends. Teapots with a story behind them make great conversation pieces while adding sentimental value to your collection. Collectors repeatedly say their most treasured teapot is the one that was tucked away in their mother's, grandmother's, or other relative's cupboard. Whether from a relative or bought from an antiques dealer, always ask where the teapot is from, how long they think the person had it, and other relevant questions.

To help remember such details about your teapots, write them on little pieces of paper and then place them inside the pot. Or, after you have researched a pot, make a copy of the information or make a note of where it is referenced and slip it into the teapot. Information inside a teapot is useful to help you remember the pattern name, purchase price, or some other small fact. This is very helpful if you decide to sell your teapot some years later.

There are computer programs for indexing collections, or you can keep handwritten records. While this is not necessary, it is a good idea to take photographs of your collection from time to time for personal records and insurance purposes. Check your policy or with your agent to find out if extra coverage is needed.

Teapots as Collectibles

Teapots make interesting collectibles not only because of their rich history but also because of the diversity in their shape and size. Teapots found in today's marketplace are also within the collector's financial reach. It is not necessary to be a tea connoisseur to enjoy teapots. Collectors are found in many countries. If you would like to meet other collectors, start by asking local antiques dealers if they know of anyone who collects teapots, and advertise in publications on collectibles.

Sample of mark on bottom of teapot: Germany, H.W. & Co. Wreath.

Impressed mark of Sadler, England.

Crown & Banner mark of Leona from Gibson's.

Sadler Backstamp from brown, red and green decoration.

What to Look For

Collectors agree that mint condition teapots are the ideal, but the fact is that teapots were designed for use and are therefore prone to chipping and crazing. It would be difficult to amass a collection containing only perfect specimens. Be sure to use special care in handling teapots you are considering for purchase. Always place one hand over the lid as you pick up the pot, preventing the lid from slipping off. Also, be aware of fragile handles – if possible, inspect for cracks before picking up a pot by the handle. Here are some common flaws and considerations for each:

MISSING LID

The possibility that you will ever find the right lid or one that fits is slim. Teapots without lids are worth very little. I do not suggest purchasing teapots without a lid except at a minimal price, for these reasons:

- for research – you have a similar pot, and the lidless pot will help you identify the other.
- it evokes sentimental feelings.
- you want to use it as a flower vase.
- you have researched the teapot and are sure it was made before 1850, adding some value.

ABOVE **Using a lidless teapot as a pencil holder.**

CRAZING

Crazing is a condition in which the glaze of the teapot, either on the inside, outside or both, has fine hairline cracks. There are two reasons for this condition:

- The clay body and the glaze were not fired at high temperatures, which gives best fusion. Any stress on the pot, such as boiling water for tea or a cold pot dunked into hot dishwater, causes the crazing.
- The teapot was dropped or bumped, causing a physical stress not hard enough to break the pot but enough to crack only the glaze.

Crazing diminishes the value of a teapot, but should not exclude it from purchase. The crazed glaze rarely chips or peels off, and often the pot can still be used. You may find teapots with only crazing on the inside and the fine cracks are stained with tea. If you are not sure, see if you can test the pot with some tepid water. While the pot is holding water, watch to see if crazing on the outside darkens. If so, the pot cannot be used for brewing tea.

Crazing on a teapot made in Japan with a red, berry-like design.

CRACKS

Fine, hairline cracks are sometimes hard to see. Examine any teapot in good lighting, and use your fingers to feel suspect areas. Hairline cracks commonly occur with use and only slightly diminish the value.

Cracks under the lid or inside the rim of the pot are acceptable. Before purchasing a teapot with noticeable cracks in the body, handle, or spout, take into consideration all other elements such as price, age, and the pot's personal appeal. It may add nicely to your collection, or you may regret the purchase.

CHIPS

Damage to teapots happens most often to spouts. They tend to stick out and get bumped, causing chips. Small chips can be repaired with success but large, missing pieces are harder to repair. Weigh the size of the chip against the overall value of the teapot. Prices should be reduced 30 to 40 per cent for chips compared with mint condition values.

Chips also occur with frequency on lids, especially the undersides, and on the rims, where lid and pot accidentally clash. Be sure to examine these areas for chips.

Weigh your decision to add a slightly damaged teapot to your collection against the following two factors. First, how rare is the teapot? Could you find it again sometime in better condition? Any mark of a manufacturer will help in determining this. And second, does the price reflect devaluation because of damage? If you are not sure, wait and try to determine this by further research and searching out other similar teapots.

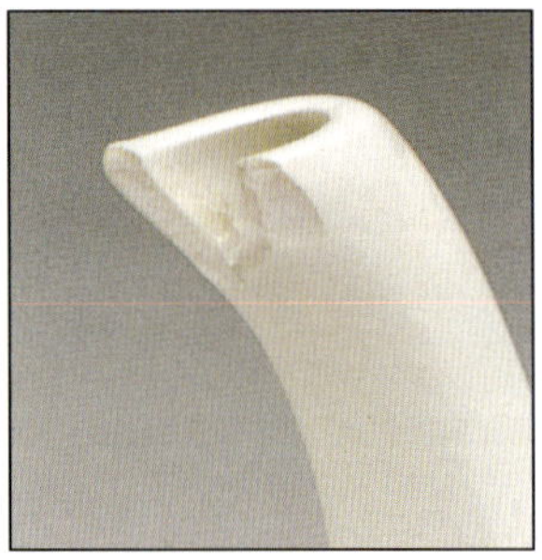

LEFT **Chipped spout on a teapot made in Ireland.**

RIGHT ***Peach stone* tea set was probably a souvenir sold in gift shops in states in the U.S.A. producing peaches. The stones are hollowed out and handles and spouts applied.**

DISPLAYING AND STORING TEAPOTS

Glass-enclosed cabinets of any kind, especially china cabinets, are perfect for displaying your teapots. Shelves installed near the ceiling also show off your collection while adding charm to any room of the house.

Groupings of a few teapots in various settings are pleasing to the eye and add to your decor. Arrange teapots with similar colours in a room with the same hues. A yellow and blue kitchen easily warms up to teapots of the same colour or those with similar colours in their decoration.

Breakable items and small children or pets do not often mix, so bear this in mind when displaying your collection. Some collectors add a small piece of floral wax to the underside of their pots to keep them from vibrating to the edge of a shelf and falling over the side. Another method is to attach a small piece of moulding along the outer edge of the shelf.

The wonderful thing about teapots is that they were made for everyday use. Do not hesitate to use your collection. The most common and a decorative way to get some miles from your teapot is to fill it with a lovely bouquet of flowers.

Small teapots are handy storage containers for things such as teabags, sugar or sweetener packets, or try one as a ring-holder near the kitchen sink. In the bathroom, teapots hold cotton balls, Q-tips, or, without the lid, your toothbrushes.

On your desk, some teapots are just the right size for pens, pencils, or postage stamps. A teapot can also be a fun place to hide your own stash of candy or tea cookies. Enjoy some of your more common teapots in everyday living, and keep those cherished heirlooms behind glass.

Useful Addresses

Teapot Collections

LONDON

V&A (Victoria & Albert Museum), Cromwell Road, London SW7 2RL, tel. (071) 938 8500. The national decorative arts collection, with extensive ceramics galleries. Exhibits from ancient times to the present day include many teapots.

Tea and Coffee Museum, 4 Maguire Street, London SE1 2NQ, tel. (071) 378 0222. A small museum displaying a personal collection of teapots, coffee pots and associated artefacts, plus displays on the history of tea and coffee.

THE POTTERIES

Stoke-on-Trent City Museum and Art Gallery, Bethesda Street, Hanley, Stoke-on-Trent ST1 3DE, tel. (0782) 202173. Displays one of the largest and most important collections of English pottery, mainly Staffordshire.

Minton Museum, London Road, Stoke, Stoke-on-Trent ST6 2DQ, tel. (0782) 292292. Museum in the Minton Factory.

Royal Doulton, Nile Street, Burslem, Stoke-on-Trent ST6 2AJ, (0782) 292292. The **Sir Henry Doulton Gallery** traces the history of Royal Doulton china and there are factory visits.

Spode Works, Church Street, Stoke, Stoke-on-Trent ST4 1BX, tel. (0782) 333466. Telephone for information about the new visitor centre and museum under construction as we go to press.

Wedgwood Visitor Centre, Barlaston, Stoke-on-Trent ST12 9ES, tel. (0782) 204218. The museum traces the story of Wedgwood from the establishment of the first pottery in Burslem. There are also factory visits, demonstrations, a cinema, and gift shops.

Contact the Potteries **Tourist Information Centre,** The Factory Shop, Quadrant Road, Hanley, Stoke-on-Trent ST1 1RZ, tel. (0782) 284600 for information on the many mills and potteries open to the public, plus factory visits.

DERBY

City Museum and Art Gallery, Strand, Derby DE1 1BS, tel. (0332) 255 586. An important collection of pottery and porcelain produced in Derby from 1750.

Royal Crown Derby, 194 Osmaston Road, Derby DE3 8J2, tel. (0332) 712800. The museum traces the history and manufacture of Royal Crown Derby pottery and porcelain.

ABOVE *Smiley face* **This pastel-coloured teapot was made in Japan in the late 1930s to mid-1940s. The whimsical features mimic cartoon characters of the era. Matching salt and pepper shakers are available.**

Denby Pottery Visitors Centre, Derby Road, Denby, Derbyshire DE5 8NX, tel. (0773) 743 644. A museum of Denby pottery, plus a craft room and shops.

Where to Purchase Teapots and Accessories

U.K.

Eliza Hurdle Ceramics, 14 Oxford Street, Kingsdown, Bristol, B52 8HH.

Swineside Ceramics, colour brochure, Leyburn, Wensleydale, North Yorkshire, DL8 5QA. tel. (0969) 23839 or Fax (0969) 24079.

LONDON

Alfie's Antique Market, 13–25 Church Street, London NW8 8EE, tel. (071) 723 6066. Britain's largest antiques market with nearly 400 dealers.

Antiquarius 135–141 King's Road, Londong SW3 4PW, tel. (071) 351 5353. A famous London antiques market with a diverse selection of china and glassware.

Gray's Antique Market 58 Davies Street, and **Gray's Mews** 1–7 Davies Mews, London W1Y 1AR, tel. (071) 629 7034. The dealers here specialize in fine, elegant decorative arts, including porcelain and silverware.

Harrods Ltd. Old Brompton Road, Knightsbridge, London SW1X 7QX, tel. (071) 730 1234. Find teapots by all the famous names in Harrods' world-famous china department.

Kensington Church Street London W8. You are sure to find some interesting antique teapots in the shops along this street of antiques shops. It is also worth calling into **Constance Stobo,** close by at 46 Holland Street, who specializes in Staffordshire pottery, and **Jean Sewell,** at 3 Campden Street, who sells 18th- and 19th-century porcelain from around the world.

THE POTTERIES

There are more than 40 factory shops selling seconds from pottery factories around the Potteries and from elsewhere in the UK. They include:

Minton House, London Road, Stoke, Stoke-on-Trent ST4 7DQ, tel. (0782) 292121. Museum in the Minton Factory.

Portmeirion Seconds Shop, London Road, Stoke, Stoke-on-Trent ST4 7QQ, tel. (0782) 411756.

Royal Doulton, Victoria Road, Fenton, Stoke-on-Trent, tel. (0782) 291 869. The **Sir Henry Doulton Gallery** traces the history of Royal Doulton china and there are factory visits.

Spode Works, Church Street, Stoke, Stoke-on-Trent ST4 1BX, tel. 0782 744011. Telephone for information about the new visitor centre and museum under construction as we go to press.

Wedgwood Visitor Centre, Barlaston, Stoke-on-Trent ST12 9ES, tel. (0782) 204218.

U.S.A.

China Specialties, request catalogue, 19238 Dorchester Circle, Strongville, Ohio 44136, tel. (215) 238–2528.

ABOVE ***Realistic conch shell* is an individual-sized teapot with a crustaceous body. The color varies from light greens to mottling and dark browns. This pot was made in Japan c.1950. Other pieces were also manufactured to match.**

The Collector's Teapot, full-colour catalogue for $2, P.O. Box 1193, Kingston, New York 12401, tel. 1–800–724–3306 ext. 72

The Hall Closet, outlet store for Hall China Company. Open Mon–Sat, 1 Anna Street, East Liverpool, Ohio 43920, tel. (216) 385–4103.

Holmes by Hall, request available Sherlock Holmes items, P.O. Box 221B, Flushing, Michigan 48433.

Horchow Home Collection request catalogue, subscription for $5.50. 2251 E. Walnut Hill, Irving, Texas 75039, tel. 1–800–456–7000.

Madame Chung Finest Teas, Inc., Catalog available. P.O. Box 597871, Chicago, Illinois 60659, tel. (312) 743–5545.

Where to Purchase Tea

L. Fern and Co., 27 Rathbone Place, London W1P 2EP, tel. (071) 636 2237. The oldest and most atmospheric Fern's, offering a small range of select teas and coffees.

H. R. Higgins, 79 Duke Street, London W1M 6AS, tel. (071) 629 2913. An elegant old Mayfair shop with a stock of choice teas, in addition to the famous range of coffees. H. R. Higgins supply teas and coffees by Royal Appointment. Mail order from 10 Lea Road Industrial Park, Waltham Abbey, EN9 1AS, tel. (0992) 768254.

The Tea House 15A Neal Street, London WC2H 9PU, tel. (072) 240 7539. A Covent Garden tea boutique offering 40+ varieties of tea plus a wild selection of novelty teapots garnered from potteries all over Britain.

R. Twining and Co., 216 Strand, WC2R 1AP, tel. (071) 353 3511. The entire Twining's range is available from this shop. There is a small museum at the back with exhibits and artefacts on the history of tea and of Twinings.

Whittard of Chelsea Ltd., Mail order sales and shop, 73 Northcote Road, London SW11 6PJ, tel. (071) 924 1888. Send for a price list for Whittard's 50 or more teas, but visit one of their many shops in central and south-west London to see the unusual teapots they have for sale.

ABOVE ***Gibson's rose-decorated teapot* was made c.1950s by Gibson's, Staffordshire, England. Gibson's have made many shapes and sizes of teapots since 1885, and are still in business.**

Further Reading

Agius, Pauline, *China Teapots,* Lutterworth Press, Great Britain, *c.*1982.

Bigelow, Francis Hill, *Historic Silver,* Tudor Publishing Co., New York, 1948.

Bramah, Edward, *Novelty Teapots,* Quiller Press, London, *c.*1992.

Clark, Garth, *The Eccentric Teapot,* Abbeville Press, New York, *c.*1989.

Cooper, Emmanuel, *A History of World* [illegible] *c.*1972 & 1981.

DeBolt, Gerald, *American Pottery Marks,* Collector Books, Paducah, Kentucky, 1994.

Huxley, Gervas, *Talking of Tea,* John Wagner & Sons, Ivyland, Pennsylvania, *c.*1956.

Kazuko, Okakura, *The Book of Tea,* Charles E. Tuttle Co., Rutland, Vermont, *c.*1956.

Kovel, Ralph and Terry, *Kovel's New Dictionary of Marks,* Crown Publishers Inc., New York, 1986.

Langford, Joel, *Silver,* Quintet Publishing, London, Chartwell Books, Secaucus, New Jersey, 1991.

Lechler, Doris Anderson, *Children's Glass Dishes, China, and Furniture,* Vol. 1 & 2, Collector Books, Paducah, Kentucky, 1991.

Masse, H. J. L. J., *Chats on Old Pewter,* Dover Publications, New York, 1971.

Miller, Philip, *Teapots and Coffee Pots,* Midas Books, Great Britain, *c.*1979.

Miller, Philip and Berthoud, Michael, *An Anthology of British Teapots,* Micawber Publications, Great Britain, *c.*1985.

Pratt, James Norwood, *The Tea Lover's Treasury,* 101 Productions, San Ramon, California, *c.*1982.

Sandon, Henry, *Coffee Pots and Teapots,* John Bartholomew and Son Ltd., Edinburgh, *c.*1973.

Street-Porter, Janet and Street-Porter, Tim, *The British Teapot,* Angus & Robertson Publishers, Great Britain, *c.*1981.

Warner, Oliver, *The English Teapot,* The Tea Centre, London, *c.*1948.

Price Guides

The following books are annual edition price guides which include a category on teapots:

Huxford, Sharon & Bob, Editors *Flea Market Trader,* Collector Books, Paducah, Kentucky.
Garage Sale & Flea Market Annual, Nostalgia Publishing Co., La Center, Kentucky.

Huxford, Sharon & Bob, *Schroeder's Antiques Price Guide,* Collector Books, Paducah, Kentucky.

Rinker, Harry Ltd., *Warman's Americana & Collectibles,* Wallace-Homestead Book Co., Radnor, PA.

Publications

The Collector's Teapot, P.O. Box 1193, Kingston, New York 12401, tel. 1–800–724–3306 ext. 72. Full-color catalog of teapots.

Mary Mac's TeaTimes Newsletter, P.O. Box 841, Langley, Washington 98260, tel. (714) 898–8562. Published 6 times per year.

Tea Talk, 419 N. Larchmont Blvd. #225, Los Angeles, California 90004, tel. (310) 659–9650. A quarterly newsletter on the pleasures of tea, including teapots.

Book Sources

Antique Publications, send for price guide, P.O. Box 553, Marietta, Ohio 45750–0553.

Collector Books, send for price list of collectible reference books, P.O. Box 3009, Paducah, Kentucky 42002–3009.

Crown Publishers, Inc., request list of collectibles books, 225 Park Avenue South, New York, New York 10003, tel. 1–800–526–4264.

House of Collectibles, request list of Official Price Guides, 201 East 50th Street, New York, New York 10022.

John Ives Bookseller, request current catalog of new and out-of-print books. 5 Normanhurst Drive, Twickenham, Middlesex, TW1 1NA, England. From U.S. telephone (011 44 81) 892 6265.

The Putnam Publishing Group, Perigee Books, request listing of Lyle Publications, 200 Madison Avenue, New York, New York 10016.

Wallace-Homestead Book Company, request price guide, Radnor, Pennsylvania, 19089.

INDEX

ACKNOWLEDGEMENTS

The author and publishers would like to thank the following individuals and organizations for permission to photograph teapots from their collections: b = bottom, c = centre, l = left, r = right, t = top. Gary Stotsky, York, Pennsylvania: p10 t, p22 t, p23 br, p25 tl, tc, p31 bl, p61 tl, p63 l, p69 br, p6 t, p7 t. The Stotsky collection was photographed by Hayman Inc., York, Pennsylvania. A&P Co, Brockton, M.A. p11 r. Sally Burkhardt, Santee, Ca. p16 b, p20 bl, p25 bc, br, p28 c, b, p35 r, p39 bl, p67 l, p73 c, p76 l. Patricia Scott German, Escondido, Ca. p1 l, p29 t, b, p39 br, p60 tl, Ja'Millie's Antique Arcade, El Cajon, Ca. p24 t. Sotheby's Inc. (New York) kindly supplied the photograph p55.